Swagga for the Soul

B. SWAGZ

ISBN 978-1-0980-5495-3 (paperback)
ISBN 978-1-0980-5496-0 (digital)

Copyright © 2021 by B. Swagz

All rights reserved. No part of this publication may be reproduced, distributed, or transmitted in any form or by any means, including photocopying, recording, or other electronic or mechanical methods without the prior written permission of the publisher. For permission requests, solicit the publisher via the address below.

Christian Faith Publishing, Inc.
832 Park Avenue
Meadville, PA 16335
www.christianfaithpublishing.com

Printed in the United States of America

To those who struggle: Your pain can either define you or it can strengthen you. Do not fall victim to the devil. Allow yourselves to fall to pieces so that God can put you back together the way *He* wants; not the way you want.

To my auntie: God has blessed me with you and your wisdom. You have never been wrong nor led me astray, and I thank you for encouraging me to do the most painful things I have ever had to do in my life. I can see why my Uncle Scott loved you so very dearly. Just as your favorite verse says, you are also a lamp to *my* feet (Psalm 119:105). I love you!

To Jennifer Kelly: Thank you for showing me *The Secret*. I am forever grateful to you!

To my readers. I would like to clarify the order of this book, as it was not written in a traditional sense. I began writing Swagga for the Soul in 2012. This was the year of my revelation revealing to me that began my journey as a Spiritual Teacher. I wrote the first chapter, Love, and I set my pen down. At this time in my life, I hadn't really experienced much of the content that I have written about in the entire book. At that point, I had been a saved Christian for ten years. It wasn't until I experienced true pain and suffering that I picked up my pen again. In 2014, at age twenty-nine, I had lost a boyfriend due to a suicidal overdose that had forever changed my life. In 2015, I found out I was pregnant with my first son, Chase. Soon after, I gained a new boyfriend, Shane (not Chase's father) and began a torturous and abusive relationship. 2015 was the year I decided to pursue my purpose for the Lord once again. I wrote most of my chapters in the summer of 2015 and concluded the book in early 2016; however, my chapters were not written in the numerical order they appear. I wrote my chapters based on what lessons I had learned according to the fruit of the Spirit in Galatians chapter five, the basis of Swagga for the Soul. Throughout this book, my age ranges from twenty-seven to thirty-two. As you read the book, my age could drastically change from one chapter to the next. The editors pointed out this flaw to me and suggested I update the information provided to be set in present time, which is now the year of 2020, the year I decided to pursue publishing this book. I declined. The purpose of this book and any book I write is to share my testimony. My testimony consists of a journey of years, and it is important for this to be recognized as we all have our own unique journeys. Life happens and when it does, it is important to recognize that it might not be over night, or over a number of weeks or months. In my case, life changing moments happened over a number of years. I apologize for any confusion this may cause my readers. Follow along with an open heart. Everything I speak is very real and very true. I am a messenger of God and mean no harm in the words I speak. The truth is what the Lord wants from all of us, and He has deemed me as a teacher to spread His word in an easy to read manner. May the Lord bless all of you on your journeys. I pray in the end that you all find yourselves with Him. God bless!

Contents

Swagga	9
Love	11
Show Some Love	15
Love the Lord	16
Love Your Neighbors	19
Love Your Friends	22
A Friendship to Avoid	24
Love Your Enemies	27
A Different Perspective	30
Love Your Parents	35
Love Your Children	38
Love Your Brethren	40
Love Your Husband	44
An Interesting Perspective	46
Love Your Wife	48
Love Yourself	50
Light It Up	56
Joy	60
Rise 'n Shine	70
Peace	75
Patience	82

Kindness	86
Quit Hatin'	87
Goodness	90
Tiger Stripes	100
Faithfulness	102
Gentleness	119
Coldhearted Christians	125
Self-Control	131
Hold Up	132
Live by the Spirit	141
Live It Up	142
B's Confession	144
B's Favorite Motivational Verse: Always Move Forward	147
Walk by the Spirit	148
Walk It Out	149
Conclusion	151
Swagga Takeaway	153
Works Cited	155

Swagga

Elegant. Beautiful. Stylish. Glamorous. Flashy. Trendy. Unique. Pretty. Handsome. Classy. Attractive. Striking. Different. Chic. Modish. Dressy. Formal. Athletic. Preppy. Vintage. Sophisticated. Skater. Quiet. Southern. Sporty. Earthy. Fancy. Simple. Plain. Emo. Ska. Punk.

B. SWAGZ

Swagga is my all-time favorite word. Wait a second, let me rephrase that…*swagga* is my favorite *non-word* word; street slang term, if you will. I love it because it pertains to who I am. It also pertains to who you are and who she is and who he is, etc. You see, we *all* have *swagga*. The world may tell you differently—on the TV, on the radio, in the magazine ads—but if the actual term is used to describe *your* individual characteristics, then don't be fooled by the world! Each and every person in this world possesses *swagga* and each of us is created so uniquely that we all flaunt it differently, as well.

According to many people in the world, *swagga* is usually defined in a physical sense by what you wear and how you wear something. But this is where the viewpoint of my book changes. What does the word *swagga* mean to the Lord? Probably nothing. He certainly doesn't judge us on the latest styles or trends we have come across. In fact, have you ever considered how God defines this word? Well, He already has! In the Bible, there are many descriptive words that the Lord may consider to be our *swagga*. Love. Joy. Peace. Patience. Kindness; Goodness. Faithfulness. Gentleness. Self-control. I believe these qualities pertain to the true *swagga* that God wants all of us to have, and they are referred to as the fruit of the Spirit (Galatians 5:22–23).

We have all heard the expression "Beauty comes from the inside." Like that, *swagga* shows more than who we are; it *says* who we are. We have one life to live and one soul to dress until judgment day. Spiritually speaking, our souls are what are accounted for in the end. Our physical *swagga* is not going to determine where we go after death. It is our *spiritual swagga* that is sought as the most important *swagga* on earth. That being said, let us focus on how God wants us to look and not on how the world wants us to look. He will bring out the most appealing *swagga* in each of us if we choose to swag ourselves out by the way *He* says rather than by what the world says. Define your soul, and let the *swagga* you possess be revealed through Him. Flaunt your inner swag…it's the only one that counts!

Love

Love is patient, love is kind *and* is not jealous;
love does not brag *and* is not arrogant, does not act unbecomingly;

It does not seek its own, is not provoked, does not take into account a wrong *suffered*, does not rejoice in unrighteousness, but rejoices with the truth;

bears all things, believes all things, hopes all things, endures all things. Love never fails; but if *there are gifts of* prophesy, they will be done away; if *there are* tongues, they will cease; if *there is* knowledge, it will be done away. (1 Corinthians 13:4–8)

Have you ever loved someone and not received the same love in return? Have you ever had your heart broken into a million pieces? It hurts, right? Have you ever considered that God's heart could break? Sadly, it does. When we turn away from Him; when we don't worship Him; when we put our desires before Him; and when we love the things of the world more than Him—these things hurt Him! God is our Creator. He is the *only* Creator of everything we see in this world. He doesn't ask for much, just to be loved. And in return, He blesses our lives with our essential needs to survive and the marvels of the world that we desire. "Ask, and it will be given to you; seek, and you will find; knock, and it will be opened to you. For everyone who asks receives, and he who seeks finds, and to him who knocks it will be opened." (Matthew 7:7–8). Doesn't it seem a little foolish to not show Him the love He deserves? I would say so! God is all about the love, so it only seems fair to show it in return.

There have been so many days in my life that I have felt so deeply alone and so unloved. Unloved—that is, by people in my present life, people from my past, and people I have hoped would love me in the future. Through my darkest days and deepest depressions, there is and always has been someone that loves me unconditionally. Every day of my life, He loves me; through all of my hardships and my struggles, He loves me; on my good days and on my bad days, He loves me; at my best and at my worst, He loves me. He loves me so, even when I choose not to love Him back. His love is always present. It is never lost; it can only be found. And He doesn't just love *me*, He loves *you*, too. Whether you have a bad day, a bad month, even a bad many years, God loves *all* unconditionally. It's the kind of love you may have felt from an animal or a pet. Animals, especially pets, have a keen sense for our emotions. Regardless of how we may have treated them in the past, pets show an unconditional love to us; a devotion to their owners. In the same manner, our Lord shows us this unconditional love. "For God so loved the world, that He gave His only begotten Son, that whoever believes in Him shall not perish, but have eternal life" (John 3:16).

God's love is not limited to those who believe. Jesus also said, "*It is* not those who are healthy who need a physician, but those who are sick; I did not come to call the righteous, but sinners" (Mark 2:17). Jesus suffered and died for every soul on this earth, for the righteous *and* the unrighteous. Why? He did this because He *loves* us! "For the Son of Man has come to save that which was lost" (Matthew 18:11). How many of us would suffer and die for someone who didn't love us? How many of us would sacrifice our child—our *only* child—to save a person who commits evil? To die *willingly* to save many people who have done evil to you or to your loved ones? I have to say that I am not too confident that I would. But God sacrificed His son, and Jesus sacrificed His life for us all because He loves us that much. That is the unconditional love we need to wear on our souls every day.

According to the Merriam-Webster Collegiate Dictionary, *love* is defined as "a strong affection for another person, especially a person of the opposite sex; an object of affection; a sweetheart; any strong liking or affection." In the back of my New American Standard Bible, *love* is defined in just two words—"compassion, devotion." God wants love to be uncomplicated for us. In fact, He wants it to be as simple as the definition listed in the concordance of your Bible. So let's break down the words He describes as love. *Compassion* is defined as "concern, love." *Devotion* is defined as "dedication; consecration; godliness; affection; love; zeal."

We are to be compassionate toward others. To *love one another,* as Jesus says in John 13:34. Notice in this verse that Jesus didn't say we are to love *some* others but *one* another, each person counting as one. We are to love God; to love our neighbors; to love our friends; to love our husbands; to love our wives; to love our children; to love our enemies. God wants us to be merciful to *everyone,* even our enemies. Love your enemies and pray for those who persecute you (Matthew 5:44). God even wants us to love things other than each other. He wants us to love good (Amos 5:15); to love to stand and pray (Matthew 6:5); to love to give (God loves a cheerful giver [2 Corinthians 9:7]). The list can go on and on.

We are also to be devout to one another, to dedicate ourselves to good deeds according to God. And not merely to friends or enemies (and everyone in between) but also to His creatures, creations, and the earthly things He approves of. We are to show affection and zeal (enthusiasm) and dedication toward the things *He* wants us to love, not the things that *we* want to love or that *someone else* wants us to love. We are to love just as Christ loved us (John 13:34).

Having love for everyone and everything that God wants us to sure seems a whole lot easier said than done. I struggle with this every day, as I am sure many of you do, too. We need to have faith that God will lead us to the love He wants us to have. We need to pray and ask God to lead us in finding that unconditional love He wants us to show in our everyday lives. God wants us to go to Him for guidance with everything we struggle with. He also wants us to be compassionate toward Him throughout our days and devoted to Him no matter what we go through. He wants us to live a godly life for Him so that He can bless us in return with *endless* blessings! Remember, struggling with something, especially with loving someone or something, doesn't make us bad people. In fact, it's the struggles that make us stronger. Be kind and compassionate to the Lord and be open to His advice in His word. He *will* strengthen your every weakness! But don't give up if your prayer for love (or anything else) isn't answered. God answers prayers in *His* time, not ours. Be patient, have compassion, and show some love to our Lord.

Show Some Love

Show some love has become quite a popular phrase in today's world, especially in terms of communication. The internet is full of sites that have popularized this phrase, especially for young people on websites such as MySpace, Facebook, Twitter, etc. If you haven't heard from a friend in a while or if you make a request to be added to someone's *friend list* online, you may see the many comments about *showin' some love.* In a worldly sense, this phrase seems to begin and end at just that—a written sentence. In a godly sense, however, showing some love requires compassion and devotion; an actual *act* of showing love. In simple terms, we are to love one another. In the Bible, God specifically addresses us to love the following—God; neighbors; friends; enemies; parents; children; brethren; husbands; wives; self. That's a lot of people to show love to every day! With our busy lives at work and at home, we are bound to ignore a lot of these people on the list. It is only human to feel many things besides love toward others. It is also very easy for us to make excuses to justify the love we don't show, like "I'm tired" or "That person deserved it" or "I'll get to that next week." But God doesn't ask us to love everyone… He *commands* us to! He not only commands us to love others, but He also commands us to have love for other earthly things that *only* He approves of. He also wants us to *not love* many things. *I* am not writing this to tell you how to love or who to love; that is not up to me. I am simply informing you of how and who *God* wants you (us) to love. Love is a learning process, and I am learning just as much as you are as I write this.

Love the Lord

"'Teacher, which is the great commandment in the Law?' And He said to him, *'You shall love the Lord your God with all your heart, and with all your soul, and with all your mind.'* This is the great and foremost commandment" (Matthew 22:36–38).

Jesus was asked this question by a lawyer of the Pharisees—a Jewish religious party—and His response to this man was as clear as day. And the same response would be given to us if we were to ask the Lord that question. We are to love the Lord with all our hearts, with all our souls, and with all our minds. We see this verse again in Mark 12:30 and added to it is "and with all your strength." God does not expect our love. He *wants* our love and *desires* our love. *He* is the one who brought each of us into the world. Yes, your parents gave birth to you, but it is *God* who brought your parents into the world to give birth to you, and their parents before that, and their parents before that, and so on. He is our true parent, our Father, *the* Father we are to love most. And His invitation to love Him extends to you and me until the day we die, but why wait? "Come to Me, all who are weary and heavy-laden, and I will give you rest. Take My yoke upon you and learn from Me, for I am gentle and humble in heart, and *you will find rest for your souls*. For My yoke is easy and My burden is light" (Matthew 11:29–30). Love the Lord, and let Him give your soul the rest it deserves.

First and foremost, God wants us to establish our love for Him. He is to come before any other living thing on this earth. He is to be our sole number one. I believe once we establish that love for Him in our own lives, everything else He has planned for us will fall into place. "And we know that God causes all things to work together for good to those who love God, to those who are called according to *His* purpose" (Romans 8:28). Without love for God, then our purpose here on earth simply has no purpose. It is up to us to show the Lord not just some of our love but *all* of our love. Through thick and thin, hard and easy, good and bad, we are to always express our love to Him. He will establish us once we establish our love for Him in compassion and devotion to His every will.

Paul writes to the Romans, "For I am convinced that neither death, nor life, nor angels, nor principalities, nor things present, nor things to come, nor powers, nor height, nor depth, nor any other created thing, will be able to separate us from the love of God, which is in Christ Jesus our Lord" (Romans 8:37–39). Do you allow things in your life to separate you from loving the Lord? Life is busy and chaotic; no argument there. But we can always love the Lord. Not one person can take that from us because our minds are our source of free will to love whom we want.

Love Your Neighbors

"O Lord, who may dwell on Your holy hill? He who walks with integrity, and works righteousness, and speaks truth in his heart. He does not slander with his tongue, nor does evil to his neighbor, nor takes up a reproach against his friend; in whose eyes a reprobate is despised, but who honors those who fear the Lord; he swears to his own hurt and does not change; he does not put out his money at interest, nor does he take a bribe against the innocent. He who does these things will never be shaken" (Psalm 15).

We learned in Matthew 22:37 of the great and foremost commandment—love the Lord your God with all your heart, with all your soul, and with all your mind. The second is like it: *"You shall love your neighbor as yourself"* (Matthew 22:39). This commandment has been long established since the Old Testament and continues to be commanded to us in the New Testament.

Now let us define *neighbor*: "one who lives near another; a person or thing next or near another; a fellow being." That being said, we should consider every individual we come in contact with to be our neighbor (even our family). Regardless of a person's reputation, appearance, wealth status, etc., remember what Jesus says, "Do not judge so that you will not be judged. For in the way you judge, you will be judged; and by your standard of measure, it will be measured to you." (Matthew 7:1–2). In the Old Testament, there were strict laws to be followed in reference to how we are *not* to treat our neighbors: "You shall not oppress your neighbor, nor rob *him*" (Leviticus 19:13). "You shall do no injustice in judgment; you shall not be partial to the poor nor defer to the great, but you are to judge your neighbor fairly. You shall not go about as a slanderer among your people, and you are not to act against the life of your neighbor; I am the *Lord*" (Leviticus 19:15–16). "You shall not hate your fellow countryman in your heart; you may surely reprove your neighbor, but shall not incur sin because of him. You shall not take vengeance, nor bear any grudge against the sons of your people, but you shall love your neighbor as yourself; I am the *Lord*." (Leviticus19:17–18). Let us remember the Golden Rule: treat others the way you want to be treated (Matthew7:12).

Here are just a few ideas of how you can show your neighbors some love:

A simple good morning; hold open a door; help unload groceries; lend a hand; smile; let the car that is blocked go in front of you; drive slow in the neighborhood; pay for the order of the person behind you in the drive-thru line; say "Thank you;" say "Please;" expect nothing in return; give your old clothes to the needy; babysit a night free of charge; donate items you no longer use; give a tissue to a person in need of it; call an old friend; make amends with your enemies; pray for the sick; give someone a hug; mail cards of cheer; remember birthdays; wait patiently in line; volunteer at a homeless or animal shelter; give at least one compliment a day to a stranger; share; wash the dishes; send flowers for no reason; visit the elderly; let a person with less items go in front of you; say "Excuse me;" be attentive to your parents; listen; give change to the poor; slow down; say "God bless you;" give hope to the hopeless.

Being a neighbor is a role God has blessed each of us to be. The opportunities to act neighborly to each other are endless. A small act of random kindness is more than enough to fulfill the duties of a neighbor. Think about how you desire to be treated, and treat your neighbors the same. "Love does no wrong to a neighbor, therefore love is the fulfillment of *the* law" (Romans 13:10).

Love Your Friends

"Greater love has no one than this, that one lay down his life for his friends" (John 15:13).

Friendship is a companionship between two or more people. Life without friends would be extremely lonesome. We have all been blessed with friendships in our lives. Not one person in this world lives without the opportunity to have a friend. "You are My friends if you do what I command you. No longer do I call you slaves, for the slave does not know what his master is doing; but I have called you friends, for all things that I have heard from My Father I have made known to you. You did not choose Me but I chose you, and appointed you that you would go and bear fruit, and *that your* fruit would remain, so that whatever you ask of the Father in My name He may give to you. This I command you, that you love one another" (John 15:14–17). What greater friend than Jesus could we ask for? No one! For no one can compare to our Redeemer who is forever loving and forgiving. Jesus will never betray us because He is a true friend. In my high school days, my dad often repeated a famous quote to me by Lee Iacocca, "When you die, if you've got five real friends, then you've had a great life." True friends are hard to come by, but Jesus is true until the end. We are to follow His example in how to be a true friend to others. "A friend loves at all times" (Proverbs 17:17). Love is a crucial component of friendship. "Therefore, be imitators of God, as beloved children; and walk in love, just as Christ also loved you and gave Himself up for us, an offering and a sacrifice to God as a fragrant aroma" (Ephesians 5:1–2).

A Friendship to Avoid

"You, adulteresses, do you not know that friendship with the world is hostility toward God? Therefore whoever wishes to be a friend of the world makes himself an enemy of God" (James 4:4).

We are also warned of a friendship we are *not* to develop. This pertains to *any* friendships with the world that are forbidden by our God. We are to guard ourselves with the love of the Lord so that we do not partake of evilness in any form.

Many verses in the Bible warn us of these evil deeds. "Do not love the world nor the things in the world. If anyone loves the world, the love of the Father is not in him. For all that is in the world, the lust of the flesh and the lust of the eyes of boastful pride of life, is not from the Father, but is from the world" (1 John 2:15–16). "Do not participate in the unfruitful deeds of darkness, but instead even expose them; for it is disgraceful even to speak of the things which are done by them in secret" (Ephesians 5:11–12). "Therefore be careful how you walk, not as unwise men but as wise, making the most of your time, because the days are evil. So then do not be foolish, but understand what the will of the Lord is. And do not get drunk with wine, for that is dissipation, but be filled with the Spirit" (Ephesians 5:15–18). "But avoid worldly *and* empty chatter" (2 Timothy 2:16).

Actually, read Galatians 5:19–21. It reads, "Now the deeds of the flesh are evident, which are: immorality, impurity, sensuality, idolatry, sorcery, enmities, strife, jealousy, outbursts of anger, disputes, dissensions, factions, envying, drunkenness, carousing, and things like these, of which I forewarn you, that those who practice such things will not inherit the kingdom of God." Wow, that's pretty much everything. No wonder it's so hard to be a Christian and why obeying God isn't taken as serious as it should be. I fail every day, I know that, but it's the *intentional* sin that is not forgiven. "For if we go on sinning willfully after receiving the knowledge of the truth, there no longer remains a sacrifice for sins, but a terrifying expectation of judgment and *the fury of a fire which will consume the adversaries"* (Hebrews 10:26–27). We all make mistakes, but we are all responsible for doing what is right. And God knows our intentions, so it's impossible to fool Him. *Fool* is an interesting word here because my Bible concordance defines it as "unwise person." If a person thinks that they can fool God, they certainly are unwise.

> "But put on the Lord Jesus Christ, and make no provision for the flesh in regard to *its* lusts" (Romans 13:14).

Love Your Enemies

"If your enemy is hungry, give him food to eat; And if he is thirsty, give him water to drink; For you will heap burning coals on his head, And the *Lord* will reward you" (Proverbs 25:21–22).

How hard is it to show an enemy of yours some love? Even as a Christian, I will admit that this is still most challenging for me. Although I have always disliked having enemies, sometimes they are just an inevitable part of my life. My auntie told me once that not everyone in the world is going to like me back, no matter how nice or sweet I am to them. It really hurt me to hear that, but I know it's something I need to accept. But just because someone doesn't like me does not mean I am to act in the same demeanor toward them. I am to show love to my enemies, no matter how hard that may be.

Jesus talks about loving our enemies in Matthew 5. "But I say to you, do not resist an evil person; but whoever slaps you on your right cheek, turn the other to him also. If anyone wants to sue you and take your shirt, let him have your coat also. Whoever forces you to go one mile, go with him two. Give to him who asks of you, and do not turn away from him who wants to borrow from you. You have heard that it was said, *'You shall love your neighbor* and hate your enemy.' But I say to you, love your enemies and pray for those who persecute you, so that you may be sons of your Father who is in heaven; for He causes His sun to rise on *the* evil and *the* good, and sends rain on *the* righteous and *the* unrighteous" (Matthew 5:43–45). It is not our job to hate those who hate us but to love those who hate us. The Lord promises He will take care of the rest.

It really takes a lot of willpower for me to resist taking revenge upon someone who has done me wrong. I believe, as human beings, we tend to have this natural reaction to just want to get even. Jesus set the ultimate example to us on how to truly resist taking vengeance upon those that caused Him suffering. He was beaten (Matthew 26:67, Matthew 27:30); spat upon (Matthew 26:67, Matthew 27:30); mocked (Matthew 27:29); humiliated (Matthew 27:28); crowned with thorns (Matthew 27:29); and crucified (Matthew 27:33–56). Through all of that and more, Jesus did not react in a defensive way. He showed even His enemies love because that's what God taught Him, and therefore obeyed the Lord to set that example to us. I encourage you to read the entire book of Matthew of Jesus and His journey all the way through to His death.

"Never pay back evil for evil to anyone. Respect what is right in the sight of all men. If possible, so far as it depends on you, be at peace with all men. Never take your own revenge, beloved, but leave room for the wrath *of God,* for it is written, *'Vengeance is mine, I will repay,'* says the Lord" (Romans 12:17–19). If then by committing evil acts unto others is wrong, according to our God, we are ultimately hurting ourselves more than our enemy when we do such things. One way we can try to overcome this temptation to pay back our enemies is to think of Jesus. What would Jesus do in a situation of confrontation…show love or show hate? He would show love and then some! It now becomes our duty to set that same example to others as Jesus did. To those of you who have never tried this concept, I can speak from experience that showing love in a situation of hate can have remarkable effects on an enemy or rival. Just a few years ago I remember having an argument with my brother—*sibling rivalry,* as my dad would call it. We were text-battling all of these mean words back and forth to each other when I realized it was not going to end if I kept responding with the (mean) things I was saying. When he had texted the statement "I hate you" to me, I thought, *Okay, I can reply with the same thing back if I really wanted to and continue this conversation for hours.* Suddenly, I recalled a verse from the Bible, "Do not be overcome by evil, but overcome evil with good" (Romans 12:21). I instantly typed a response for him in my phone, "I love you." The argument had ended. Did I really just win the battle? I realize now that the fight was never between me and my brother. It was between the Lord's love and the devil's hate. Will every fight dissipate by love? Yes. "Hatred stirs up strife, but love covers all transgressions" (Proverbs 10:12). Will it always work on the first try? You will never know unless you try. "All things are possible to him who believes" (Mark 9:23), but we must have patience just as the Lord is patient with us.

A Different Perspective

I became very close with a family from church that had moved to Cleveland from Texas. Zeth and Jade both attended Texas A&M University in College Station, Texas, which is home to the Texas A&M Aggies. When the family returned to Texas for the winter, I had the privilege of visiting them there. We took a drive around the university which is the main attraction in town. Jade explained to me that A&M is a school of traditions and values, many dating back to the late 1800s. The tradition that really stood out to me was the one pertaining to the Aggie football games. The Aggies, including students, fans, faculty, etc., do not *boo* at their opponents. I thought to myself, *Wow, are you serious?* I did my research at home and came to understand that the stadium, Kyle Field, is capable of holding a number of around 86,000 people. This meant no negative comments, no objects being thrown, and no booing. From a crowd of that size, it is really astounding to me that this happens. And it happens at every single home game. How amazing is that? That really displays a sense of humbleness and love toward an enemy.

Unfortunately, the rest of us in the world don't necessarily follow those rules. We are naturally, in a sense, very competitive, especially when it comes to sports. Supporting your home team is an extremely common standard to live by in most, if not all, societies. So how do we overcome such common everyday standards? One thing we can do is change our perspective. Like the family I knew in Texas, learning about something new and different compared to the norm really opened my eyes to see that despite competition, love and respect can still be shown. And then I came to realize that in a godly perspective, it *should* be shown to everyone no matter what the circumstances. Remember, just because someone is an *enemy* does not mean that we should treat them as an enemy according to how the world would, but rather we should show an enemy love just as Jesus did.

Revenge. This is a hard temptation to resist. I struggle with it, do you? Or have you in the past? Revenge is a natural defense mechanism for many of us. When a person makes us mad, we want to make them mad right back, am I right? This can be face-to-face; while we're driving; through emails and texts; over the phone; behind others' backs; any way, really. Revenge is a result of anger. It could also be from resentment, hatred, jealousy, etc., but anger is certainly the root. The Lord makes it clear in the Bible that He does *not* like anger and, therefore, we are to not be angry. I take that back. We can be angry. After all, we are human and imperfect. However, we are not to show our anger. *"Be angry, and* yet *do not sin;* do not let the sun go down on your anger, and do not give the devil an opportunity" (Ephesians 4:26–27). A verse that comforts me when I ponder upon revenge is this: "For we know Him who said, *'Vengeance is mine, I will repay.'* And again, *'The Lord will judge his people.'* It is a terrifying thing to fall into the hands of the living God" (Hebrews 10:30–31).

Anger can lead to countless opportunities for us to sin. From using curse words to committing murder, anger can lead to anything but good. How often do we see horrid acts of crimes, murders, robberies, etc. on the news? These things ultimately stem from some sort of anger. Perhaps a person hated another person and committed murder to them or someone else. Or maybe a person was angry that they couldn't afford the nice things they see that others have so they decide to rob a bank. Anger doesn't necessarily mean anger. There are many other words to describe anger. To better understand this, here are twenty synonyms of anger: animosity, annoyance, displeasure, distemper, enmity, fury, hatred, impatience, indignation, infuriation, irascibility, ire, irritability, mad, outrage, petulance, resentment, soreness, temper, violence (thesaurus.com, 2012). A person can simply be annoyed to become angered, have displeasure with something, or resent someone. We must learn to control our anger because this is what the Lord says we are to do. "Let all bitterness and wrath and anger and clamor and slander be put away from you, along with all malice. Be kind to one another, tender-hearted, forgiving each other, just as God in Christ also has forgiven you" (Ephesians 4:31–32). "A fool always loses his temper, but a wise man holds it back." Can anger show love? Absolutely not. "If hate stems from anger, there is no room for love to grow" (B. Swagz).

There is only one on this earth who can show His anger and that is the Lord our God. In the Old Testament, the Lord demonstrated his wrath many times in many ways. Several examples of whom God was angry with include Moses (Exodus); Jonah (Jonah); David (1 Samuel); Job (Job); and the entire Israeli nation (Exodus). I have seen some really angry people in my past (and I have been a really angry person in the past) and cannot fathom being on God's bad side and seeing the wrath of *His* anger. His anger would make the angry people I have seen look like saints with glowing halos. That can't be good! If you are as scared as I am of the Lord's anger, then you are right where you belong. We are to fear the Lord and His anger which, I believe, is the main point of the Bible. I mean, we aren't supposed to fear *Him* (because He is truly an awesome God!) but rather fear the consequences of disobeying Him. I know I'm scared. I have been through so much in my life, as we all have. Can you imagine living at the lowest point you have ever been forever and ever times 1,000,000? That's how I view hell. I am terrified—just *terrified*—to live in my deepest, darkest pain forever, so I try and try and try to do what the Lord instructs me to do. If I weren't scared, I would, for sure, do anything I wanted to all the time. Unfortunately, a lot of people don't fear the Lord's consequences. I sure hope this book finds you and gives you a red flag as to not continue a life of intentional sin. At least, do me a favor and remember the worst moment of your *entire* life. Do you ever want to feel that way again? I sure hope not. So to my Christian swaggers, encourage the people you love and care for to consider living their earthly life for God. You're going to hear the response "You only live once" like a broken record, but please don't give up on them. Persistence is key, and like my friend Janey says, "All you have to do is plant the seed."

Ha-ha, so here's one for you. I was writing yesterday. On a roll. I mean, absolutely inspired by God to write. I went back to it today to get it ready to finally print out the first chapter of Love, but guess what? It didn't save! Talk about the devil tempting me to be angry, right? I didn't give in, though. I don't know how. All I thought was, *Well, I can write this as an example in my anger section. Lol. We have to see the positive in everything.* So I guess I have to rewrite all that I wrote. Luckily, I remember pretty much everything I wrote but it won't be exactly the same. Maybe it'll be better. Maybe God thought, *No, Brooke. Redo it!* Ha-ha, that'd be quite comical. Okay, here it goes…

Getting back to God and how He has the power to be angry goes as far back as man was created. And by the way, there are many, many, many examples of God and His anger in the Bible, I'm just mentioning a few! He got mad at Adam and Eve for eating from the tree of knowledge of good and evil. In Genesis 3:14–19, God reveals His anger and the consequences for disobeying Him. Then there is the story of Cain and Abel; the story of Noah and the flood (which I wrote such a good piece on yesterday!). Actually, yeah, I'll go ahead and try to rekindle what I wrote about Noah. You see, God was so angry with mankind that He destroyed the earth! Do you know how lucky we are or have been that He hasn't destroyed the earth because of our wrongs? Extremely blessed! "Then the Lord said to Noah, 'Enter the ark, you and all your household, for you *alone* I have seen to be righteous before Me in this time.'" Noah and his wife, their three sons, and their wives were the only ones saved, along with the animals that God told Noah to fill the ark with. How blessed was Noah and his family; how unfortunate were the ones left behind? Wow, I wrote this so much better yesterday, so bear with me. In the end, God promised to never destroy the earth again with *water,* meaning we're not off the hook. God will destroy the heavens and the earth again. "But the day of the Lord will come like a thief, in which the heavens will pass away with a roar and the elements will be destroyed with intense heat, and the earth and its works will be burned up" (2 Peter 3:10). I don't know about you, but I certainly don't want to be a part of that! Point being, don't be angry and don't give God a reason to be angry with you.

> "Do not be eager in your heart to be angry, for anger resides in the bosom of fools" (Ecclesiastes 6:9).

Love Your Parents

"Children, obey your parents in the Lord, for this is right" (Ephesians 6:1).

Love your parents. This seems like it would be a natural, easy rule to live by, right? Of course, we all go through the different stages of life when we love our parents; hate our parents; disobey our parents; and eventually respect our parents. Did you know that we are commanded to *honor* our parents? As the Fifth Commandment in the Old Testament, it is written, "Honor your father and your mother, that your days may be prolonged in the land which the Lord your God gives you" (Exodus 20:12; Deuteronomy 5:16). Many more verses in the Old Testament testify the importance of this commandment: "Hear, my son, your father's instruction, and do not forsake your mother's teaching" (Proverbs 1:8); "A wise son makes a father glad, but a foolish son is grief to his mother" (Proverbs 10:1); "A wise son *accepts his* father's discipline" (Proverbs 13:1); "A wise son makes a father glad, but a foolish man despises his mother" (Proverbs 15:20); "A foolish son is a grief to his father, and bitterness to her who bore him" (Proverbs 17:25); "A foolish son is destruction to his father, and the contentions of a wife are a constant dripping" (Proverbs 19:13); "He who assaults *his* father *and* drives *his* mother away is a shameful and disgraceful son" (Proverbs 19:26); "Listen to your father who begot you, and do not despise your mother when she is old" (Proverbs 23:22); "He who keeps the law is a discerning son, but he who is a companion of gluttons humiliates his father" (Proverbs 28:7); "He who robs his father or his mother, and says, 'It is not a transgression,' is the companion of a man who destroys" (Proverbs 28:24).

We can find more verses in the New Testament of the Bible which is the *new law* that we are commanded to follow by our Lord. "Children, obey your parents in the Lord, for this is right. *Honor your father and mother, so that it may be well with you, and that you may live long on the earth*" (Ephesians 6:1–3). Also, "Children, be obedient to your parents in all things, for this is well-pleasing to the Lord" (Colossians 3:20–21). "In all things" is quite significant. This may apply to countless situations, such as divorce; alcoholism; wealth status; drug abuse; falling away from the Lord; commitments of adultery; addictions of any kind; failure to succeed; abandonment of their child/family; failure to love and preach the Word of God; and so on.

And to my Christian girlies out there, *son* and *brother* don't insinuate that we're off the hook. The Bible refers to all of us, so no excuses, 'kay? You can't go to God on the day of judgment and say, "Well, that's not fair. I didn't know you were instructing girls, too." Lol, sorry!

God is our Father...we need to respect Him and all that He tells us to do.

To sum up the *love your parents* section, love your parents at all times! Just as God loves us daily, *no matter what*, we need to focus on His love and how He wants us to show our love through the good and bad.

And just as our Father above is patient with us, we need to be patient with our parents in the same way. I know it's hard to live at home with your parents for so long. I am twenty-five now and still living at home, and let me tell you, it is a challenge every day for me to love and respect my father. I'm not going to lie; I get quite frustrated with him all the time! I get grumpy, irritable, rude, mean (he just called me a *meanie* last weekend!), annoyed, embarrassed, pretty much all the ways you can feel about a parent. Sometimes I react in the wrong way (snap on my dad or lash out in anger) and that leaves me feeling bad and guilty after all he has done for me in my life. So I suppose one key to loving your parents is to just try and keep on trying! Being in the adolescent stage of life is so tough, and we all experience it as we grow. Reading and understanding the Bible and what it says about loving our parents is an excellent way to relieve our daily anxieties and/or frustrations we may have with our mothers and fathers. I believe another thing that can help us is to sit down and talk with our parents. To tell them about our good days, our bad days, what stresses us out, what makes us mad, what makes us happy, and what they can possibly do to help us avoid situations that can end in bursts of anger. We all have our lists of pet peeves that drive us crazy about this person or that person, especially our parents, but, remember, you and I both have pet peeves that drive our parents and others crazy as well! Let me close this section by sharing a *swagga* secret for the soul: love and *be* loved. Can't go wrong with that!

Love Your Children

"Behold, children are a gift of the Lord, the fruit of the womb is a reward" (Psalm 127:3).

It is more than a privilege to procreate. Having children is like having a lifelong pet, but it is up to each of us to raise our *pet* in such a way that love is *always* present. Not just any love but a godly love. This godly love is unconditional and, more importantly, teaches children at an early age how to truly show love to one another. I babysat for quite a few families from church in my twenties, and there were two girls in particular that I observed as behaving much different than the others. Not to say that the other parents didn't raise their kids in love, but these girls seemed as if they were taught more often than others how to love and be respectful to others according to God. Now, parents, please don't take offense to this! It is important that I make this point for God's sake rather than my own. And also for the next generation of parents that they seek advice from God on how to raise their children rather than from a magazine, talk show, or library book. God knows best when it comes to children. Do you know why? Because *we* are His children! He created us in love and wants each of us to grow in that love every day of our lives, from the time we are born until the day we part from this earth. Why? Because He loves us so! So it is absolutely crucial that we follow the teachings of the Lord to teach our own. And who better to learn from than our parents? If God is our parent to begin with, then it makes perfect sense to continue following His teachings and pass them on to the children we bore through Him.

Love Your Brethren

"But we request of you, brethren, that you appreciate those who diligently labor among you, and have charge over you in the Lord and give you instruction, and that you esteem them very highly in love because of their work" (1 Thessalonians 5:12).

How great is family? I absolutely love mine! Even if I don't see them as often as I would like, it sure is comforting to know that they are there. Some people aren't as fortunate to have a biological family, and my heart truly goes out to them. Did you know that when you are baptized into Christ and become a member of *His* church, you become a part of *His* family? This family is known as your brethren and it is like no other. Therefore, we are to love our brethren as Christ loves us.

The word *brethren* refers to brothers (and sisters) in Christ. Do you understand what that means? It means that as long as you are a member of Christ's church, then you have this extended family of brothers and sisters *everywhere* in the world! Now that is a comforting thought! My brother Jack often goes out of state to take tests for different fire departments. Renting a car and staying at a hotel can be quite costly if you do it often. Jack will go online and locate a church in the area he is traveling to. Once he locates the church, he contacts the preacher and informs him of his upcoming visit. Being his brother in Christ, the preacher welcomes him to his home as if he is a part of his own family. There is no inconvenience involved. A brother offers another brother a place to stay, period. If the preacher cannot do it, then he contacts members of the church that are more than willing to offer their hospitality. How great is that? Who knew that people who have never met can show such love?

In Romans 12, the subtitle reads *Dedicated Service* (NASV). The whole chapter instructs us on how to act toward one another as members of Christ's church. We are to be devout to one another in brotherly love (verse 10); fervent in spirit and serving the Lord (verse 11); rejoicing in hope, persevering in tribulation, and devoted to prayer (verse 12); contributing to the needs of saints and practicing hospitality (verse 13).

A lot of people feel that they do not need to go to church to be spiritual. First of all, many letters written by Paul and Peter and John in the New Testament are specifically addressed to churches aka brethren aka congregations. Second, God wouldn't have given us the commandment to love our brethren if He didn't want us to go to church. "We know love by this, that He laid down His life for us; and we ought to lay down our lives for the brethren. But whoever has the world's goods, and sees his brother in need and closes his heart against him, how does the love of God abide in him" (1 John 3:16–17)? Lay down our lives for the brethren… Wow. To put this phrase in another perspective, would you lay down your life for your family? For your mother or father, brothers or sisters, aunts and uncles, nieces or nephews? If you have a strong relationship with anyone in your family, I am quite certain you would answer yes to this question, as would I. Third, what is the point of having churches (Christ's church, Matthew 16:18; not to be confused with a denomination) if our intentions are to abstain from them? I got nothing.

One more example I would like to share with you in regards to loving your brethren. My dad, whom I love so dearly, has complained over the past year about a specific someone at the church that he goes to. For the most part, I would listen to him venting and nod in agreement. However, after hearing about it every Sunday and every Wednesday, I just couldn't take it anymore. I finally blurted out, "Um, aren't we supposed to love *all* of our brothers?" (I even knew a verse to point out to him if he argued: 1 John 3:15, "Everyone who hates his brother is a murderer; and you know that no murderer has eternal life abiding in him"). I think he just agreed with me to end the conversation, but my point is that if we do not love each other in the church, then how are we supposed to go into the world and preach love to non-Christians? Not to say that I am a saint; I have struggled with this myself and have learned that nothing good comes from hatred or animosity. By disliking these individuals, I gave myself no opportunity to show them love. One of my favorite catch phrases is "Kill 'em with kindness." If I show them the love that the Lord wants me to show them, then maybe I wouldn't have an excuse to dislike them. I am one to take things very personally, so when I feel that I am being mistreated by someone, it really just eats away at me and causes this wrath inside of me. That's bad! I don't want that for me, and I don't want that for you. Having hatred toward anyone in the brethren can also result in a fatal decision—to withdraw from the church.

We are to love our brethren as our family because they are simply that—family. More importantly, they are our brothers and sisters in Christ. Being a part of a brethren has its share of responsibilities. The first, of course, is to love your brothers and sisters. "Be devoted to one another in brotherly love" (Romans 12:10).

Love Your Husband

"For the husband is the head of the wife, as Christ also is the head of the church, He Himself *being* the Savior of the body" (Ephesians 5:23).

It seems to me that one of every two families is divorced. If my guess is correct, then that is a sad, sad statistic. As women, we are so unbelievably blessed to have the chance to have a husband in our lives. It is more than a privilege to join together with a man to become one. God knew this from the beginning as He created man *first*. "The LORD God formed man of dust from the ground, and breathed into his nostrils the breath of life; and man became a living being" (Genesis 2:7). Both a husband and a wife have responsibilities to fulfill. "To the woman He said, 'I will greatly multiply your pain in childbirth, in pain you will bring forth children; yet your desire will be for your husband, and he will rule over you'" (Genesis 3:16). Marriage isn't perfect; only Jesus is perfect. For wives, it is probably very hard to accept that the husband is, in fact, in charge. A sense of control may overcome wives and push them away or instill a resenting anger toward them. God didn't make this command of letting the husband rule for nothing. Man came first, so naturally he is the dominant gender. In chapter five of Ephesians, the New American Standard Bible has a heading above verse 22 that reads, *Marriage Like Christ and the Church*. The verses that follow say, "Wives, be *subject* to your own husbands, as to the Lord. For the husband is the head of the wife, as Christ also is the head of the church, He Himself *being* the Savior of the body. But as the church is subject to Christ, so also the wives *ought to be* to their husbands in everything" (Ephesians 5:22–24). This is not to say that husbands are always right in everything they do or say. It simply means that wives should be willing to obey their husbands as we are to obey Christ, giving them the same respect and honor as we do to Christ. Our loving Savior commands this for our benefit and it should never be viewed as a disadvantage in a marriage. Wives, your *swagga* is to show your husband love, honor, respect, and submissiveness through every step of your marriages, regardless of the fights, arguments, or anything else that may come between you throughout your lives. Try to view disagreements as a test to build your endurance throughout your marriage and to come to a better understanding of your role as a wife. Tests and trials and hardships are going to happen; not giving up is your lifelong vow to your husband. Love it and appreciate it every day until death do you part. Vows are said for a reason. Commit to these vows as you commit to the Lord.

An Interesting Perspective

I heard something the other day. A friend of my brother's got married (yay!). Here's the catch—it was a fixed marriage. A lot of nationalities choose this way of life which is fine—you know, to each their own. What really got to me, though, was my brother's comment. He pointed out that even though their marriage is fixed, the couple makes it work because, according to their religion (or whatever set of rules they have), they *have to* make it work. They cannot opt out, so to speak. So I thought, *Wow, if a couple that met on their wedding day can make a marriage work, why can't couples that have been together for years make it work?* The wife then has to learn to love, honor, and respect her husband. This, in turn, can make the couple stronger in love and recognize their roles in the marriage. It baffles me that couples that have been together forever refuse to respect their significant other in the way that our Lord instructs us to. This is where reading the Word is so important. It tells us about the game of life and the rules to play it. All we have to do is follow the instructions.

To close this section, I will end with my absolute favorite passage of the Bible that is titled *Description of a worthy woman*. It is in the thirty-first chapter of Proverbs starting with verse ten and goes until the end of the chapter. It reads, "An excellent wife, who can find? For her worth is far above jewels. The heart of her husband trusts in her, and he will have no lack of gain. She does him good and not evil all the days of her life. She looks for wool and flax and works with her hands in delight. She is like merchant ships; she brings her food from afar. She rises also while it is still night and gives food to her household and portions to her maidens. She considers a field and buys it; from her earnings she plants a vineyard. She girds herself with strength and makes her arms strong. She senses that her gain is good; her lamp does not go out at night. She stretches out her hands to the distaff, and her hands grasp the spindle. She extends her hand to the poor and she stretches out her hands to the needy. She is not afraid of the snow for her household, for all her household are clothed with scarlet. She makes coverings for herself; her clothing is fine purple. Her husband is known in the gates, when he sits among the elders of the land. She makes linen garments and sells *them*, and supplies belts to the tradesmen. Strength and dignity are her clothing. And she smiles at the future. She opens her mouth in wisdom, and the teaching of kindness is on her tongue. She looks well to the ways of her household, and does not eat the bread of idleness. Her children rise up and bless her; her husband *also*, and he praises her, *saying:* 'Many daughters have done nobly, but you excel them all.' Charm is deceitful and beauty is vain, *but* a woman who fears the Lord, she shall be praised. Give her the product of her hands, and let her works praise her in the gates."

There are a number of verses within that passage that I like, but the one that I believe personally that especially applies to a good wife is in verse 25, "Strength and dignity are her clothing, and she smiles at the future." To me, those two things are crucial in succeeding at a wife's role within her household. May the Lord be with all of you, wives, in everything you do and in every way you approach your husband. If your love is surrounded by the Lord, then His light will shine through you.

Love Your Wife

"Wives, *be subject* to your own husbands, as to the Lord" (Ephesians 5:24).

I have yet to become a wife, but I often read about a wife's role and her duties to her husband according to God. We can see that God created man on the sixth day (Genesis 1:27). God was so thoughtful that He didn't want man to be alone. He then brought a deep sleep upon Adam, and as he slept, the Lord took one of his ribs and fashioned it into a woman (Genesis 2:18–23). Reading on, verse 24 says, "For this reason a man shall leave his father and his mother, and be joined to his wife; and they shall become one flesh." Although men are the head of the household, wives are to be loved by their husbands, just as Christ loved the Church (Ephesians 5:25).

A few more important instructions written to husbands are written in various places in the Bible. One important commandment directed toward husbands is found in the Ten Commandments in the book of Exodus. In verse 17, it reads, "You shall not covet you neighbor's wife." The same concept also applies to women. In Matthew 5:31-32, it reads, "It was said, 'WHOEVER SENDS HIS WIFE AWAY, LET HIM GIVE HER A CERTIFICATE OF DIVORCE,' but I say to you that everyone who divorces his wife, except for the reason of unchastity, makes her commit adultery; and whoever marries a divorced woman commits adultery." *When Jesus speaks in all capital letters in the Bible, it is of greater importance. In other words, He* really *means business!* Another place in the New Testament (the law we are all under and expected to obey) is found in 1 Corinthians 7. Starting with verse one, it reads, "Now concerning the things about which you wrote, it is good for a man not to touch a woman. But because of immoralities, each man is to have his own wife, and each woman is to have her own husband. The husband must fulfill his duty to his wife, and likewise also the wife to her husband. The wife does not have authority over her own body, but the husband *does*; and likewise also the husband does not have authority over his own body, but the wife *does*." Marriage is the unity of a man and woman, and they are to become one. Husbands (and man in general) are to look at no other women besides their wives, for this is considered adultery in the Lord's eyes (Matthew 5:28).

Love Yourself

"Do you not know that you are a temple of God and *that* the Spirit of God dwells in you? If any man destroys the temple of God, God will destroy him, for the temple of God is holy, and that is what you are" (1 Corinthians 3:16–17).

How can we love others if we do not love ourselves? How can we show our spiritual swag to others if we do not love ourselves? It would be quite hypocritical, don't you think? I have struggled with this a great deal of time in my life. I still struggle with it. Being a girl, especially, it is difficult to love ourselves in this day of age. The media fills our minds with what is and what isn't attractive and that anything else is unacceptable. We are to love ourselves and envy no one. The word *envy* in the back of my Bible's glossary is defined in one word—jealousy. Again, the world makes it nearly impossible to not feel jealous. There are so many materialistic things of this world that we are drawn to. I get jealous of lots of things; the things I don't have, that is, from the finer things that money can buy us (like fancy cars, big houses, expensive garments, etc.) to the exquisite beauty of models and celebrities in magazines and on TV. I like how a rap artist defined jealousy in a song, "But jealousy is just love and hate at the same time." That's so true. So by envying someone, you are causing yourself to love them and hate you, right? That's not cool. God doesn't want that for you or me or anyone because He knows how miserable that would be. God doesn't want us to be miserable, remember that!

Envy, when used as a verb, is defined as "discontent." We can't love ourselves if we are not content with who we are and what we have. If we love the Lord and choose to live the godly lifestyle which He desires, then we have to be content with all of the conduct of being a Christian. "Do not let your heart envy sinners, but *live* in the fear of the Lord always" (Proverbs 23:17). This means that we shouldn't feel as if we're missing out on all of the fun that we used to have. I was literally just on the phone catching up with an old friend. He asked about who I hang out with now and if I still hang with anyone we used to back in the day. I told him that I don't hang out with anyone anymore, I just hang out with my family because if I go back to my old friends, then I *will* go back to my old life of sin. But I was completely content with admitting that because I desire the godly life over my past life of sin. But say I were to respond in a resentful way (in regards to my Christianity), saying things like "I wish I didn't have to do what's right" or that "I wish I was out doing the (bad) things I used to do" or that "I dearly miss my old life and old friends"…that is not being content with the Christian that I am. On the other hand, Paul speaks about contentment in such situations, "Therefore, I am well content with weaknesses, with insults, with distresses, with persecutions, with difficulties, for Christ's sake; for when I am weak, then I am strong" (2 Corinthians 12:10). We have to be content with who we are spiritually, first and foremost.

We should also be content with our physical appearance. This is a tough one for me because I was raised by a mom that worshiped the term *skinny*. I mean, to this very day it is embedded in my brain that I need to be skinny and anything less (or more actually, lol) is unacceptable. True story—my mom just got back from San Diego a couple of weeks ago. She bought me a shirt from the Hard Rock. It's super cute and in my favorite color—mali-blue. I finally put it on today to wear and I decided to take a picture and send it to her so she could see it in use. Ten snapshots later, I deleted every picture. You know why? Because I feared my recent weight gain would strike her attention more than the fact that I'm wearing the shirt she got me. So I get that it's extremely hard for some of us to be content with our physical selves. So here's something I have to keep telling myself even if I don't get it—if I set my mind on the things above—i.e., heaven—rather than the things on this earth—i.e., being skinny—then it doesn't matter what I look like because once I die my soul flees from my body, anyway. So why is it so hard? I guess I'll have to keep praying about that.

We absolutely need to learn to be content with what we have. Again, this one is super hard for me. I constantly focus on the things I don't have and the things I wish I had when, really, I have more than I should have and more than I deserve. Paul speaks in Philippians 4:11-12 "Not that I speak from want, for I have learned to be content in whatever circumstances I am. I know how to get along with humble means, and I also know how to live in prosperity; in any and every circumstance I have learned the secret of being filled and going hungry, both of having abundance and suffering need." If you know anything about the apostle Paul, you will learn that he went through a lot. He was arrested, beaten, starved, and really suffered a whole lot of hardship. The book of Acts tells about him most and his sufferings, so for him to be content is really amazing. How many of us could be content after going through all of that? We need to think about the good and leave the bad behind. Be content with what we have and stop worrying about what we don't have or where we don't live or what we can't do. Besides pleasing God, being content is an awesome feeling. I'm not there yet all the way, but the more I write and the more I study and the more I live for God the more at ease I feel with everything that's going on or has gone on in my life. Hope you give it a shot.

As much as God wants us to love, there are also a number of things that we are commanded *not* to love. Yes, that's right, even after that whole big list I mentioned that we are to love. We are not to love the world or the lusts in it (1 John 2:15–16); we are not to love evil; we are not to love idols; we are not to love money (1 Timothy 6:9–10); we are not to love false doctrines or false prophets (Matthew 24:11 and Matthew 24:24–28). Jesus comments on the love of wealth in Matthew 6:24 which reads, "No one can serve two masters; for either he will hate the one and love the other, or he will be devoted to one and despise the other. You cannot serve God and wealth." Have no fear, though, for God has clearly written all of the things we are not to love in His holy Word. He does not say these things to be mean. He says these things because He *loves* us! He wants us to live for Him and to love the way He teaches us to love so that we may live eternally with Him. What a loving God we truly have, and I so hope you appreciate that as much as I do.

> "Do not love the world nor the things in the world. If anyone loves the world, the love of the Father is not in him. For all that is in the world, the lust of the flesh and the lust of the eyes and the boastful pride of life, is not from the Father, but is from the world. The world is passing away, and *also* its lusts; but the one who does the will of God lives forever" (1 John 2:15–17).

Perhaps the hardest act of showing love is letting go. Sometimes the romantic part of love you desire simply isn't there for a person you dearly care for. That's not to say you don't want to love that person, but God may have a different person in mind for you. Remember, life is about what God wants, not what you want, especially when it comes to marriage. But just because you let them go doesn't mean you don't care for them. Look at letting go as a positive aspect; you love a person so much you're willing to let them go, if it's God's will for you. It's a really hard and sad thing to do. Props to those that have done it.

Letting go doesn't just pertain to romantic love, though. This could mean letting go of a person, people, a group of friends, or things pertaining to your old life of sin. But do not mistake letting go for losing. It may indeed feel like you are losing a lot of things when you let go of parts of your old life—friends, habits, addictions, loves, comfort zones—but our Lord above recognizes our longings and wants to replace them with better, more godly things to fill the voids we feel we are missing out on throughout our lives. Losing the world and gaining the Lord *is* winning, no matter how hard it hurts to let go. "For whoever wishes to save his life will lose it; but whoever loses his life for My sake will find it. For what will it profit a man if he gains the whole world and forfeits his soul? For the Son of Man is going to come in the glory of His Father with His angels, *and will then repay every man according to his deeds,*" (Matthew 16:24–27). God is a mighty comforter. We need to trust in Him and have an attitude of patience, thanksgiving, and love.

Then there is perhaps the most amazing act of love that I have seen from another person. I once dated a boy named Eric. Eric was the sweetest boy ever. He treated me like a princess for a little over three years. Unfortunately, my heart didn't feel the same way for him. I tried so hard to love him back. I was, however, in love with the way he treated me. I did not want to commit to him in marriage, but I did not want to let him go. To make a long story short, I followed my heart and broke up with him. Two months after our breakup, I noticed I was missing my blender. I texted Eric and asked for it back, and he was quick to answer: "Too bad." This really upset me, so I went over to his house and decided to get it back myself. He was not at home, but I let myself in with the key. To my surprise, there was a pile of folded clothes on the table topped with another girl's personal items. Filled with hurt and fury, I snapped and lashed out in anger, trashing every room in the house.

Needless to say, Eric came home to a house of havoc. When Eric arrived home, I was already back at my house. He convinced me to come back to his house to help him clean up. I knew in my head it was a bad idea, but I decided to return to his house to help him. When I returned, I set my keys inside, and he took them and ran outside and proceeded to call the police. Infuriated, I chased him in the yard to get my keys back. Not only did I fail to obtain my car keys, but I also punched him in his arm. When the police arrived, I told them Eric's dog was wanted for biting someone in the past and that the dog needed to be removed from his house.

Anyway, the point of my story about Eric is this: through all of the chaos and drama that I caused on this day, he forgave me. He even apologized to *me,* and he told me that what I did was not my fault and that we all make mistakes. What a beautiful person who knows how to *show some love.* It was so hard to let Eric go, especially after his kind heart forgave me, but I am grateful that I did because it led him to his future wife, whom he is now happily married to.

Thank you, Lord, for giving me the courage to let go of this man as it was not Your will for me to be with him.

If you are struggling to let go of someone or something that you know is not in accordance with God's will, ask our Lord for strength and comfort, and He will help you through it just as He did for me.

Light It Up

"Your word is a lamp to my feet and a light to my path" (Psalm 119:105).

The above verse was my uncle Scott's fave. Miss and love you. RIP <3

As disciples (students/learners) of the Lord, we absolutely *need* to set the best example that we can to others by glorifying God in everything we do. If others are doing wrong, maybe they aren't aware of what is right. As God guides us in what we do, we are to guide others to the Lord by lighting their way.

I am totally obsessed with lights—Christmas lights, candle lights, black lights, neon lights, and especially glow sticks (ha-ha, for those of you that know me, you know I'm a bit ridiculous with those!). Regardless of the type, all lights provide us with some sort of guidance. Think about all of the different lights we might encounter in a single day—sunlight, moonlight, streetlights, stoplights, headlights, brake lights, office lights, building lights, candle lights, flashlights, refrigerator/freezer lights, microwave lights, oven lights, lights in our homes, lights from our TVs, computers, and cell phones, and tons more that I forgot to mention. In one way or another, these lights guide us in what we do and where we go. Without these lights, we really wouldn't know what to do or where to go.

Now that we know that all lights serve a purpose, we can ultimately conclude that light is good (except when you have a migraine. Sorry, Jaiden!). "In the beginning, God created the heavens and the earth" (Genesis 1:1). It goes on to say, "The earth was formless and void, and darkness was over the surface of the deep, and the Spirit of God was moving over the surface of the waters" (Genesis 1:2). Can you guess what God created next? Yes, light! "Then God said, 'Let there be light,' and there was light" (Genesis 1:3). But why? "God saw that light was good; and God separated the light from the darkness. God called the light day, and the darkness He called night. And there was evening and there was morning, one day" (Genesis 1:4–5). Several verses later, starting in verse 14 until verse 19, God made the sun and the moon and the stars in the heavens to give light on the earth (paraphrased). How bad would it suck to be in complete and utter darkness? Would totally suck, right? Yaaas!

"I am the Light of the world; he who follows Me will not walk in the darkness, but will have the Light of Life" (John 8:12). He is the true Light (John 1:9). It would be pretty silly to say that God is darkness, and I sure do pray for those that think that. If God were darkness, then what is Satan…the light? Umm, no. That makes absolutely no sense and is straight up an insult to God (okay, B, chill out and refer to the anger section in Show Some Love!). My bad, guys! On that note, here are some verses to shed light on (no pun intended, ha-ha):

> "This is the message we have heard from Him and announce to you, that God is Light, and in Him there is no darkness at all" (1 John 1:5).

"This is the judgment, that the Light has come into the world, and men loved the darkness rather than the Light, for their deeds were evil. For everyone who does evil hates the Light and does not come to the Light for fear that his deeds will be exposed. But he who practices the truth comes to the Light so that his deeds may be manifested as having been wrought by God" (John 3:19–21). (Note: these words were spoken by Jesus.)

Okay, okay, B, so how do we *light it up?* Let's read these verses first: "You are the light of the world. A city set on a hill cannot be hidden; nor does *anyone* light a lamp and put it under a basket, but on the lamp stand, and it gives light to all who are in the house. Let your light shine before men in such a way that they may see your good works, and glorify your Father who is in heaven" (Matthew 5:14–16). So, for one, we are not to hide our light. If someone asked you for a light because they couldn't see, would you give it to them? I am so hoping you would say yes! So why not share our *spiritual light,* as well? And we should be lighting the way for everyone, not just the people we choose to.

Next, we are to let our light shine in such a way that others can see our good works. This one is tough, guys! I constantly struggle with this. I mean, all the freakin' time! Maybe you let your light shine in front of your family, then when you're out with friends, your light goes out. Maybe you're good with your friends but not your family. Or maybe you're like me and struggle with both. Whatever the case, we Christians need to work on this because, besides the Bible, *we're* the light to direct others to our loving Lord; those of darkness cannot lead others to the light.

Third, we are to glorify our Father in heaven. This is when the WWJD (What Would Jesus Do) phrase comes in handy. Ask yourself, would Jesus do this? If so, then it is glorifying. If not, well then it probably doesn't…don't you think? Oh, wait, I found a verse for this: "For you were formally darkness, but now you are the Light in the Lord; walk as children of Light (for the fruit of the Light *consists* in all goodness and righteousness and truth)" (Ephesians 5:8–9). There we go.

I think we should all ask ourselves two questions: "Do we want to go to heaven?" and "Do we want others to go to heaven?" I answered yes to both, did you? I hope so. Knowing that then, we need to let the Light of the Lord shine through us to light the way for others, especially those that are in the darkness. We were all in the darkness before we became Christians. Don't wish that upon anyone and *light it up!* ☺

Joy

"Make my joy complete by being of the same mind, maintaining the same love, united in spirit, intent on one purpose" (Philippians 2:2).

Joy is an incredible word defined as "delight, happiness" in my NASV concordance. If the definition is that incredible, imagine how it truly *feels!* We have all experienced it at one point in our lives, even if we do not remember those joyous feelings. I would say that children present the most joy in their attitudes because they are so unaware of the chaos of this world when they are so young. So why does this feeling become so hard to feel as an adult? It is because we are now so completely aware of all the distresses in life; the fears and doubts we may have about the present or future; experiencing losses through breakups, deaths, moves, evictions, job losses; debt; addictions—basically anything that can cause our emotions to get tangled up into *anything* but happiness. God didn't put us on this earth to experience the negativity that surrounds us. He wants us to be happy and joyous *all the time,* even *through* the negativity. The problem is that many of us lack the most joyous thing in life—God. Without God, joy isn't really possible. People can pretend they are happy from material items or money or their significant others, etc., but without God there is inevitable conflict with all of those things. We must find joy in the Lord so that we can find joy in all of the little things in our lives.

I just began a writing activity with my auntie that I purchased online from an amazing author that created this *Ancient Manifesting Ritual* (Sarah Prout), and I literally just finished writing down fifty-five times in a row how joyously grateful I am for something that hasn't even came true yet! We need to *feel* joy in our minds, bodies, and souls at every given moment in our lives. As the law of attraction states, "What you think about, you bring about" (The Secret, 2006). As I said before, all of our joy must start with God. He has brought every good thing into this world, including all of us. The devil will try every which way to rob us of our joy and happiness so we need to have our guards up always! I will share with you my true joy, and we will look at some examples in the Bible.

Perhaps the greatest joy I have ever, *ever* come to experience in my life came to me on November 20, 2015 at 2:22 a.m.—the birth of my precious baby boy, Chase Maddix. For those of you that do not have children, you may not understand or relate to my joy and that is okay. Read my example and think about something in your life that has brought you to that same place of extreme joy. My son is eight months old now. Every day with him is an amazingly happy experience for me. He turns my dark into light. In my darkest moments and saddest days (which I still have on a daily basis at times), his innocent face takes all of my pain. He brought me even more joy on the day I found out I was pregnant with him, and let me tell you why. Not even a year after I had lost the love of my life to an overdose suicide, I met Chase's father, who also caused me a great deal of pain in a short amount of time. He promised me the world, and I fell for it. He even took me to look at engagement rings. He was quite the deceiver, to say the least, and left me feeling so lost and hopeless. The night before I found out I was pregnant, I had decided I no longer wanted to live due to the constant breaking of my heart. I had a plan, but before carrying out that plan, I cried out to the Lord and cast out all of my anxieties one last time. The Lord heard my prayer that night. He spoke to me and said, "Brooke, do not give up hope now. Something will change in your life tomorrow, so please hang around for one more day." I decided to listen and went to bed that night and woke up. I had remembered that I was supposed to get my period. I was very regular—to the day, in fact—so I *knew* if I didn't get it that day, then I should take a pregnancy test. Four positive tests later, I rejoiced in this moment uncontrollably and was so gracious to my God above. I felt such an immaculate feeling of happiness; a desire I had been seeking for a very long time. I knew without a doubt that this child was my angel sent by God and that this baby had already changed my life forever. It was all about him from that point on. Chase turns nine months old in eight days, and I still feel the same amount of joy for him in every moment that I look at him, hold him, feed him, and comfort him. God showed me what true joy feels like through my son. He brought me to a place I do not remember ever experiencing as a child. This happiness exceeds any feeling in the world, and I wouldn't trade it for anything. I only hope to feel this way for *everything* in my life, even when I am down and out. If joy on earth can feel like this, I cannot imagine what heaven feels like!

Unfortunately, life can get in the way of our happiness—bills and expenses; our jobs; addictions; mental health issues, such as depression or anxiety; worrying about our futures; deaths of loved ones; breakups or divorces; lack of employment or losing our jobs; fears; failures. So many obstacles are thrown our ways that deter us off the path of happiness. We need to find joy in *every* obstacle! I am a huge fan of Pinterest and I am constantly reading motivational quotes. I will share some of my favorites with you:

"I can choose to let it define me, confine me, refine me, outshine me, or I can choose to move on and leave it behind me" (Anonymous)

"And I quote…your worst battle is between what you know and what you feel" (4uquotesru.com).

"Sometimes in life, your situation will keep repeating itself until you learn your lesson" (curiano.com).

"Every single thing that has ever happened in your life is preparing you for a moment that is yet to come."—Anonymous

"Fear makes the wolf bigger than he is" (German proverb).

"Everything you've ever wanted is on the other side of fear" (Anonymous).

"Throw me to the wolves and I will return leading the pack" (Anonymous).

"The problem is not the problem; the problem is your attitude about the problem" (Captain Jack Sparrow).

"The best view comes after the hardest climb" (Anonymous).

"Do not pray for an easy life, pray for the strength to endure a difficult one" (Bruce Lee).

"Don't quit. Suffer now and live the rest of your life as a champion" (Muhammad Ali).

"Broken things can become blessed things if you let God do the mending" (Anonymous).

"The 3 Cs of Life: choices, chances, changes. You must make a Choice to take a Chance or your life will never Change" (quotediary.me).

"When something bad happens you have three choices. You can either let it define you, let it destroy you, or you can let it strengthen you" (Anonymous).

"The darkest skies produce the brightest stars" (Anonymous).

Those are just a few of hundreds of quotes I pin weekly. I encourage you to find your favorites and read them daily and imbed them into your brain that you (we) are worthy of happiness every single day of our lives. If something went wrong in your life, *learn* from it. Let your weaknesses motivate you to become stronger! The Lord gives us trials to increase our faith in Him. He allows tribulations in our lives to conquer those trials with goodness. And to those of us that blame the Lord for being dealt a hand in life that is not fair, I urge you to reconsider who is to blame. The Lord *never* puts things in your life that you do not wish for, rather He allows things to happen in our lives because we have our self-will and He cannot interfere with that. It is *Satan* that tempts us, *not* God. God always allows us the *choice* to give into temptation or not. "No temptation has overtaken you but such as is common to man; and God is faithful, who will not allow you to be tempted beyond what you are able, but with the temptation will provide the way of escape also, so that you will be able to endure it" (1 Corinthians 10:13). Please do not blame God for mishaps in your life. Take responsibility for your actions and choose the path of righteousness when you are in a tempting situation. Another favorite verse of mine: "Enter through the narrow gate; for the gate is wide and the way is broad that leads to destruction, and there are many who enter through it. For the gate is small and the way is narrow that leads to life, and there are few who find it" (Matthew 7:13–14). Believe you can and resist the devil when he tempts you. You are stronger than you know.

Another thing that can seriously damage your happiness is living with, dating, or being married to a drug addict or alcoholic. Even being friends with an addict can wreak havoc on your soul. A dear friend of mine has expressed to me how unhappy she is because her husband is an alcoholic. This woman has been in my life for sixteen years. She has the kindest soul and sweetest heart I have come to know. Her wisdom is my guide along with the Lord's, as if she is His personal angel for me on earth. To hear her express to me that she is not happy saddens my heart deeply. While she is always giving me advice on how to let go of past loves and how to overcome my depression, I feel compelled to offer her my thoughts on this subject. She may not like what I have to say (at least, one particular thing I will tell her), but I pray she finds comfort in the Lord and follows His plan for her, for the Lord could never wish unhappiness upon such a beautiful soul. I have two points I would like to make to my friend, as well as anyone else who may find themselves in a situation like this (or something similar):

Number one: an alcoholic or addict will never change unless *they want to change*. It is the saddest fact in the world, as I, myself, have tried to reach out to two different addicts in my past and failed. Not that they are selfish, deceiving, manipulating, or horrible people, but their *addiction* blocks them from being the person God created them to be. No amount of love or kindness or words of wisdom can convince them to give up their habit. It is up to them and *only* them to conquer their demons. Reaching out to them is all that we can do, but when our happiness is robbed from caring for that person to the point where we can no longer feel even the slightest bit of joy in our everyday lives, then it may be time to move on without them.

    Number two: we need to be careful in who we choose as our significant others. I am not sure if my friend was aware of her husband's alcoholism prior to getting married, but tying the knot with an alcoholic or drug addict is *not* a good idea, to say the least. Once you marry someone, that is an agreement *for life*. God does not like divorce, so why put yourself in a situation to allow even the thought of divorce to cross your mind? With alcoholics and addicts comes distrust, resentment, regret, hurt, lies, pain, deceit, manipulation, laziness, failure to commit, lack of money, irresponsibility, unhappiness. This is why I am thirty-one and single. I *refuse* to settle for someone that could possibly cause me to divorce them. Why? Because God *hates* divorce and honestly does not allow it, except for two reasons— the act of adultery or death. "And I say to you, whoever divorces his wife, except for immorality, and marries another woman commits adultery" (Matthew 19:9). And stated in Matthew 5:32, "But I say to you that everyone who divorces his wife, except for *the* reason of unchastity, makes her commit adultery; and whoever marries a divorced woman commits adultery." I would love to tell my friend to divorce this man so that she can be truly happy in life and not have to worry about things getting done around the house or money that could be spent on providing for her family (or herself, for once) instead of his habit. I truly feel that she deserves to be happy, however, I do not believe in divorce because the Lord disproves of it so I may not offer that advice to her. Of course, my friend could make the choice to divorce him, but it comes with one consequence that she would have to abide by in order to reserve her spot in the Lord's kingdom one day (however, I am *not* God and cannot say if He would actually keep her from heaven for this. He is the ultimate judge; I am just the messenger). As that verse I just quoted in Matthew 19 says, you cannot divorce unless immorality (cheating) was involved, otherwise you cannot get remarried to another or you will be considered an adulteress in the eyes of the Lord which is very, very bad. In the Old Testament, the consequence of committing adultery was death. "If *there is* a man who commits adultery with another man's wife, one who commits adultery with his friend's wife, the adulterer and the adulteress shall surely be put to death" (Leviticus 20:10). Today, in the New Testament, we are warned of God's judgment of adulterers which could result in a spiritual death (which, to me, is far more terrifying than a physical death). "Marriage *is to be held* in honor among all, and the *marriage* bed *is to be* undefiled; for fornicators and adulterers God will judge" (Hebrews 13:4). Even if you feel you are a saint in this world, when we appear before the Creator who sentences us to eternal life or death, I imagine all of us on our hands and knees begging for forgiveness. I encourage my friend to pray to the Lord and ask Him what she should do and how she can find her true happiness in life—if she is meant to walk with this man in life drained and unhappy or if there is a different path for her to choose. I only wish her the best of joy in all the days of her life. <3

It is ironic for this friend of mine to feel this way, as just this past weekend when I visited her, she was giving me the advice to leave behind this boy I have been pursuing for fifteen months now who is also an addict. She said, "You are playing the role of the man, providing for him when he should be the one providing for you." I took her advice and ran with it. I blocked all contact with this boy once and for all. So when she told me how she was feeling about her husband, I replied, "Wow, you are just like me to Shane." She replied, "Yes, and that is why I told you to get out of that so that you don't have this as your life." I am truly praying for you, my dear friend. I love you. xoxo

I can truly empathize with anyone that is in a relationship (whether romantic or friendship) with an addict. I have fallen in love with two addicts, J and Shane. I lost J to an overdose suicide in August of 2014 (his anniversary is in fourteen days). God knows I tried my hardest to save him from his addiction. The second, Shane, whom I just left a few days ago (the absolute hardest thing in the world to do!) is an addict, as well (you will learn more about him throughout the book, especially in the "Goodness" chapter). His addiction, I must say, is much worse than J's and makes him the most evil being a girl could ever encounter. I tried even harder with this guy to help him overcome his love for drugs, but, like I said, it doesn't matter what I do or say to this guy, it is *his* decision, and as my auntie says, it is his journey. If you know or love or care for someone that is battling an addiction (or you are struggling with it yourself), pray for them! Pray not only that they may come to put an end to their habit, but ask God to give them the desire to live a godly life and to serve Him and *not* the devil. Prayers really do go a long way, so stay consistent in them and never give up hope that God will intercede one day. And if God doesn't help them because of the whole self-will thing that He cannot control, then do not take out your anger on the Lord. He came to rescue the sick and died for *all of us*, including addicts. However, he gave us the ability to choose to serve Him or give into temptation. Stay strong in your prayers and may your addicted loved ones surrender to our great and awesome God.

In closing, I will leave you with a very comforting set of verses that I have often turned to in times of distress. It is labeled, *The Cure for Anxiety:*

> "For this reason I say to you, do not be worried about your life, as to what you will eat or what you will drink; nor for your body, *as* to what you will put on. Is not life more than food, and the body more than clothing? Look at the birds of the air, that they do not sow, nor reap nor gather into barns, and *yet* your heavenly Father feeds them. Are you not worth much more than they? And who of you by being worried can add a *single* hour to his life? And why are you worried about clothing? Observe how the lilies of the field grow; they do not toil nor do they spin, yet I

say to you that not even Solomon in all his glory clothed himself like one of these. But if God so clothes the grass of the field, which is *alive* today and tomorrow is thrown into the furnace, *will He* not much more *clothe* you? You of little faith! Do not worry then, saying, 'What will we eat?' or 'What will we drink?' or 'What will we wear for clothing?' For the Gentiles eagerly seek all these things; for your heavenly Father knows that you need all these things. But seek first His kingdom and His righteousness, and all these things will be added to you. So do not worry about tomorrow; for tomorrow will care for itself. Each day has enough trouble of its own" (Matthew 6:25–34).

Now go out and use your pain and your struggles as your motivation to get your *godly* life together.

Rise'n Shine

I want to help you find some joy in your life. As a *huge* believer in the law of attraction, I believe what you think about each and every moment has an immense effect on what you attract in your life. We need to shift our thinking from *what has been* to *what could be* and *what will be* with daily positivity and affirmations of gratitude. Are you ready to rise each morning and shine for the Lord? Live with me in a day and feel your worth and happiness, even if it seems nonexistent in reality.

Every morning you wake up, be thankful! Thank the Lord for the day and the happiness it has *already* brought you. Notice how I spoke that in the past tense. Have faith that your happiness is coming and believe you have already received it. How can we get the motivation to do this every day? A friend told me he puts his keys under his bed every night, and every morning that he wakes he gets down on his knees, not to grab his keys but to *pray!* I think that is brilliant! If keys aren't the motivator, then replace them with something else. Suggestions: slippers, your favorite coffee mug, your phone, a favorite book, the Bible, the TV remote, your iPod, your shoes. You can put anything under the bed that you will need, so that when you do need that certain something, you have no excuse to not say a prayer while you are in the kneeling position.

Another friend of mine started what we call *grateful sessions*. Each day, we say what we are grateful for just through text messages. We have been consistently doing this since we met five months ago. Sometimes we say things we are grateful for in the moment, in the day, in the past, or in the future. We act as if we have received the blessings we pray upon. We truly tune into what we have been blessed with and what we want to be blessed with. My friend, Kay Mystic, crossed my path when I came across an article she wrote online. I was very down at the time, and in her article, she said to email her if I needed any advice. So I did just that! She responded immediately, and we were instant friends. Five months later, we are best friends that never even met! When I poured my heart out to her that first day, she encouraged me to recognize the things in my life that I was grateful for, even though I felt awful at the time. She said it was important to be consistent. She challenged me to do this for thirty days. She reminded me a month ago that we've been going four months strong. I was, like, "No way!" Being grateful for what you have and what you want is a perfect way to feel joy, no matter what you may be experiencing in your present life.

    Meditate! I have not mastered the art of meditation by any means, if even the slightest, but meditation to me is simply *alone time*. One of my nightly rituals is to take a bubble bath and listen to music in candlelight. The aroma of vanilla bubbles while listening to my favorite tunes is music to my ears. What is something you like to do while you are alone? Suggestions: drink a cup of coffee to the sunrise, bird watch, walk the dog, watch a thunderstorm, sing, dance, exercise, read, walk, run, breathe, walk on the beach, walk in the woods, make a collage, go to the library, window shop, take a nap. As long as you are doing something that allows you to think (or not think, if you wish to clear your head), then the possibilities are endless. Meditation does not have to be sitting Indian-style with your hands in the air with your fingers clasped, humming out loud for an hour. If that is your preference, then go for it (and more power to you!). Just find something that puts a smile on your face. ☺

    Make a to-do list each night before bed and wake up early to get your stuff done. When I was extremely depressed after I lost my boyfriend, J, I would literally sleep *all day long*. It was interfering with my health, my social life, and my well-being. My auntie told me to make a list of things to do to get my butt out of bed each day. She said to pick at least one thing off the list to do, even if it is just for an hour. Here is the exact list I made: wake up early; write in journal;

take walks; take pictures; buy new makeup; clean room; study; go to the library; visit friends; do hair and makeup daily; brush the cats; think positive; eat good; have lunch with people from church; read the Bible; pray; meditate; stretch; paint nails; buy flowers for bedroom; send cards to people; take deep breaths; go to bed early; don't look for love (lol); be happy; splurge on a new shirt; play the claw machine; window shop; make someone a gift or collage; clean the house; feel pretty; buy a new purse; get new music; find babysitting jobs. I will never forget the motivation that list gave me to get up and get moving. It truly saved my life, and I am forever grateful to my auntie for that. She has truly worked wonders in my life with all of her love, support, guidance, and wisdom. I encourage you to make a list (you can just make one big list and choose from it daily or make one each night) and start shifting your energy into accomplishments, even if they are just little ones. Remember, it takes *small* steps to make *big* changes in your life. Dare to start *now*!

Make a vision board. I got this idea from the book *The Secret* by Rhonda Byrne, and not only is it a great motivator but it is also an extremely fun process. You do not have to be an artist or even creative to make a vision board. You simply put on the board what you want in your life, such as a dream house, a new vehicle, to live on the beach with palm trees, to travel, to start your own business, anything you desire! My sister-in-law does hers a little differently. She only puts words of positivity or quotes that she lives by. I like to put pictures on mine because it takes me to that place of imagination where I really feel as if I have received all that I put on there. And that is the next step—*feel* as if you have or are receiving the things you wish for in your life. If it is a new car, then pretend you are driving it. If you desire endless money, then *feel* the abundance in your life (as opposed to feeling down from the bills that just came in the mail). I really encourage every person to read *The Secret*. I promise it will work magic in your life and bring you things you never dreamed of having. I have attracted many things in my life through the process of visualization. Some people may laugh at you and say to stop living in a fantasy world because that is what it is, in a sense. Do not listen to those people, for those are the people that will block all the good things from coming into your life. Surround yourself with positive people, positive vibes, and positive attitudes, and feel what you wish to feel for real one day. It is possible! I have read the book *The Secret* several times and the basic concept of it is *faith*. Have faith and believe you can receive all good things and you *will* receive them. Remember what I said about God's timing. He works in His time, not yours. Be patient, and in the meantime, make a vision board. Happiness is in the making!

Commit to daily affirmations of gratitude. Being grateful for the things in your life is so important! God appreciates gratitude. And to those of us that were raised with manners, saying "Thank you" is quite simple and is usually an automatic response. We say "Thank you" when we receive a compliment, when a door is held open for us, when we are given a present. I am an over thanker, lol. I tend to say "Thank you," like, five times for the same thing. Start saying "Thank you" every day under your breath for the things you are truly grateful for. "Thank you for the roof above my head" "Thank you for my family" "Thank you for my job." Say these to yourself and God. And while saying those affirmations, feel the joy of those things you are grateful for.

We can also feel grateful for things we have not received but wish to receive in our futures. "Thank you for my new car!" "Thank you for my dream home!" "Thank you for my dream job!" Feel the joy these things bring you as if you have already received them. Shift into the most grateful being you can be and smile in the process. Much like the visualizing process, we must *feel* the joy of having what we desire in the future in the present. It may take a while to get used to, but once you train your mind to feel and attract what you want in your life, God will shift His ways toward you and bless you in abundance in whatever it is that you desire.

We can rise each day and truly shine with the right attitude. Conquering our demons and battling our struggles can deplete our souls. We need to rise *above* them! We need to shine like stars! Do not let cloudy days steal your sunshine forever. God wants to give you the world, if you'll let Him. Pray to Him. Be thankful to Him. And shine for Him. Follow His light and He will shine on you! A favorite scripture of my dear auntie seems fitting here, "Your word is a lamp to my feet and a light to my path" (Psalm 119:105). And another one of my absolute favorite quotes, "Stars can't shine without darkness" (Anonymous)

Peace

"Depart from evil and do good; seek peace and pursue it" (Psalm 34:14).

Peace = calmness and tranquility

B. SWAGZ

I don't know about you, guys, but I get so caught up in this fast life I forget to just chill out sometimes. And to be honest, I don't even know what to write about in this chapter. Hmm…so not calm right now! Lol. Okay, we'll just start with some verses and I'll go from there:

> *"The one who desires life, to love and see good days, must keep his tongue from evil and his lips from speaking deceit. 'he must turn away from evil and do good; he must seek peace and pursue it. "for the eyes of the Lord are toward the righteous and his ear attend to their prayer, but the face of the Lord is against those who do evil""* (1 Peter 3:10).

I think the number one thing Christians should be at peace with is that we're forgiven of our sins, and, second, if we live a faithful life, we are blessed with a beautiful home in heaven. How can that not bring peace to someone's mind? Instead of fearing hell and stressin', we can just chill and smile at our reward. And if you're not a Christian, aren't you scared of your spiritual destination? *Or* are you at peace with where you'll end up? For my people that say "I'm a really good person and God knows that," as a child of God, I'm here to teach you the truth to that and many other non-Christian claims. Ready? That's simply not enough. There's no peace to be found if you're not of Christ. None, if you're not living in Christ. And this is all from God, I'm just the messenger. People don't want to think about hell because at church we're often taught how awesome God is. And He is awesome, that's for sure, but we need to read the fine print of the scriptures 'cause they tell it how it is, whether you believe it or not. And here to back up the whole "I'm a good person, that's good enough" statement, you need to read this: "But are you willing to recognize, you foolish fellow, that faith without works is useless" (James 2:20)? It mentions Abraham and that his faith was perfected through his works. Verse 24 says, "You see that a man is justified by works and not faith alone." And here we go, verse 26 says, "For just as the body without *the* spirit is dead, so also is faith without works is dead." We can't count on how *we* feel about ourselves because we're not judging ourselves in the end… **God is.** So if you're not a Christian, I fully encourage you to become one. You will find peace and comfort in knowing the promises of His kingdom. If you are a Christian, we need to take a minute to examine where we stand in God's eyes. Would God send you to heaven according to your faith and good works? When we are confident of these two things, that's when we can find peace. Don't stress…chillax!

Things we can take peace in:

1. Christ died for us;
2. Christ came to rescue not just the righteous but the unrighteous;
3. God does forgive when you die for Him; and
4. Going to heaven.

1. Christ died for us

The fact that Jesus died for us (sinners) definitely brings peace to my mind. Every day I think, *Wow, thank goodness He died to wash away my sins 'cause I don't want to spend an eternity in suffering.* Want to know what helps me to strive to have faith and do good works? I look back at my deepest, darkest times in my life and envision those very moments as my hell. If I were forced to relive all the horrible times I've experienced for an eternity, I would lose it! That's just crazy talk! Think about the lowest you've ever felt. Want to relive that every day and every night for the rest of time? I sure hope not. Add to that equation whatever hell will look and feel like (whatever that may be). Insane! Peter talks about a new heaven and earth, reminding us of what lies ahead for us:

2 Peter 3

> This is now, beloved, the second letter I am writing to you in which I am stirring up your sincere mind by way of reminder, that you should

remember the words spoken beforehand by the holy prophets and the commandment of the Lord and Savior *spoken* by your apostles.

Know this first of all, that in the last days mockers will come with *their* mocking, following after their own lusts, and saying, "Where is the promise of His coming? For *ever* since the fathers fell asleep, all continues just as it was from the beginning of creation." For when they maintain this, it escapes their notice that by the word of God *the* heavens existed long ago and *the* earth was formed out of water and by water, through which the world at that time was destroyed, being flooded with water. But by His word the present heavens and earth are being reserved for fire, kept for the day of judgment and destruction of ungodly men.

But do not let this one *fact* escape your notice, beloved, that with the Lord one day is like a thousand years, and a thousand years is like one day. The Lord is not slow about His promise, as some count slowness, but is patient toward you, not wishing for any to perish but for all to come to repentance.

But the day of the Lord will come like a thief, in which the heavens will pass away with a roar and the elements will be destroyed with intense heat, and the earth and its works will be burned up.

Since all these things are to be destroyed in this way, what sort of people ought you to be in holy conduct and godliness, looking for and hastening the coming of the day of God, because of which the heavens will be destroyed by burning, and the elements will melt with intense heat! But according to His promise we

> are looking for new heavens and a new earth, in which righteousness dwells. Therefore, beloved, since you look for these things, be diligent to be found by Him in peace, spotless and blameless, and regard the patience of our Lord *as* salvation; just as also our beloved brother Paul, according to the wisdom given him, wrote to you, as also in all *his* letters, speaking in them of these things in which are some things hard to understand, which the untaught and the unstable distort, as *they do* also the rest of the Scriptures, to their own destruction. You therefore, beloved, knowing this beforehand, be on your guard so that you are not carried away by the error of unprincipled men and fall from your own steadfastness, but grow in the grace and knowledge of our Lord and Savior Jesus Christ. To Him *be* the glory, both now and to the day of eternity. Amen.

Back to verse 14, "Be diligent to be found by Him in peace, spotless and blameless." Do you think this could also mean that our faithfulness gives the Lord peace? For sure! We are His children, and He wants nothing but the best for us. ☺

The book of Romans is phenomenal, and I encourage you to read it. "But God demonstrates His own love toward us, in that while we were yet sinners, Christ died for us. Much more then, having now been justified by His blood, we shall be saved from the wrath *of God* through Him" (Romans 5:8–9).

2. Christ came to save the unrighteous. Unrighteous = evil

We are all unrighteous, meaning that we are all sinners. We are the very reason that Christ died. He wants to save *all* of the unrighteous and become righteous through Him. The Pharisees asked disciples of Jesus a question in Matthew. "Why is Your teacher eating with the tax collectors and sinners?" Jesus heard this and said, "*It is* not those who are healthy who need a physician, but those who are sick. But go and learn what this means: *'I desire compassion, and not sacrifice,'* for I did not come to call the righteous but sinners" (Matthew 9:12–13). He didn't die for the good. He died for the bad. Why? Because there is no good, except for Him. May we all find peace and comfort in our flawless Lord and Savior Jesus Christ. ☺

3. God forgives us when we die in our sins for Him

"In Him we have redemption through His blood, the forgiveness of our trespasses, according to the riches of His grace which He lavished on us" (Ephesians 1:7–8).

Does God forgive? Absolutely. Jesus's blood covers all of our sins. But remember, if we do not believe in Christ Jesus, then it doesn't pertain to us. If we are believers and are *intentionally* sinning, then we can go ahead and put the word *not* after *absolutely*. It is *not* the concept of some religions' *once saved always saved*. Sorry to break that to those of you who believe that. Remember James 2:20, faith without works is useless! Great effort is required to earn the forgiveness of our God. Why? Because He says so!

"For He rescued us from the domain of darkness, and transferred us to the kingdom of His beloved Son, in whom we have redemption, the forgiveness of sins" (Colossians 1:13–14). I hope we all find peace in this because it's totally awesome!

4. Going to heaven

What do you think of when you think of heaven? For me, it's no more tears because God knows I've shed too many on this earth. I am so at peace with that. Revelation 21 describes *the new heaven and earth* written to the seven churches of Asia by the apostle Paul. Not sure if this is the heaven we look forward to, but it sure does paint a beautiful picture of it. ☺

Peace may seem impossible to find in this crazy world, but when you're with the Lord, all things are possible…even peace. Take comfort in the amazing things Christ has done for us. Count your blessings and thank Him in advance for future blessings. The ultimate goal in this game of life is to meet Him in heaven. May peace be with you always.

Patience

"The Lord is not slow about His promise, as some count slowness, but is patient toward you, not wishing for any to perish but for all to come to repentance" (2 Peter 3:9).

This is the fifth chapter I have rewritten in this book. *Fifth chapter!* Talk about needing patience—lol—but that is not the type of patience I want to focus on in this chapter. Yes, being patient with yourself and with others is important. However, being patient with *God* and *His plan* for each of us truly takes the cake on this topic. It is so easy to give up and give in when times are tough. *Believe me,* I know! But God gives us His word that if we are patient we will be rewarded. Holding on and persevering and moving forward is the key to God's plan. For you and for me. He will not let us down, and it's time we start believing in that and give Him the patience He deserves after all the patience He has with us. Ready for that miracle in your life? It is coming! "Ask, and it will be given to you; seek, and you will find; knock, and it will be opened to you. For everyone who asks receives, and he who seeks finds, and to him who knocks it will be opened" (Matthew 7:7–8).

I want to start by asking you two questions: how many years have you been graciously blessed with on this earth and how many mistakes have you made during that time period? I will tell you my answers. I have been alive for thirty-two years next month, and I have probably made almost thirty-two million mistakes (roughly a million a year!). Okay, maybe not that many mistakes. But the point of my over exaggeration is that I have made more mistakes than I can possibly count. Now, has God struck me down with lightning or condemned me to death or taken my eyesight for every mistake I have made? No. We are not living in the Old Testament days when those three things *could* happen for real for just *one* single mistake. Thank God for that! God has an incredible amount of patience with us. Just as the verse beneath the title says, "God does not wish for *any* of us to perish." He wants us to repent of our sins and live for Him so that He can reward us here on earth and in heaven. I do not know anyone in the entire world that possesses that kind of patience with one person, let alone every single soul on this earth. God is so great for that!

I have been told by many, many of my brothers and sisters in Christ to be patient with the Lord. That was a really hard thing for me to do when I found my boyfriend dead two summers ago. That was the most trying time in my entire life. I tried to escape this life two times within the first two months of J being gone. I laid in my bed all day every day; so depressed, hopeless, and faithless that I could ever be happy again in my life. I stopped going to church and didn't answer my phone when the elders called to see how I was doing. I felt like I had absolutely no purpose in my life and decided God did not love me as He says He does. Let me tell you that I was so wrong about everything! When God allowed me to see that little angel in my ultrasound seven months later, I knew that God was with me. My son, Chase, has saved my life multiple times since the day I found out I was pregnant. Had I known that God was going to bless me with him after losing a boyfriend at twenty-nine years old, I never would have doubted Him. But that's the thing. I didn't believe I would get better or be happy again because I didn't see those changes in my life right away. I gave up the day J died and refused to be patient with God's plan to pull me through. I eventually returned to church and confessed to my brethren of my pregnancy, and they welcomed me back with open arms and tears of joy. Just like the myth of Santa Claus—seeing isn't believing; believing is seeing. That, my friends, I truly believe is what patience with God is all about.

Lastly, I want to address those of you that feel you are constantly patient and waiting on God's blessings, yet are still waiting. Well, there is one very important part to asking for and receiving blessings from our Lord. Can you guess it? Yes, you must be a believer. One that follows the Word and not a denomination (manmade) organization. False prophets are everywhere, so you must be sure you are of the same church as Christ established. "I also say to you that you are Peter, and upon this rock I will build My church; and the gates of Hades will not overpower it" (Matthew 16:18). Notice that verse is Christ speaking directly to Peter, and He says *My* church, not the pope's, not the preacher's or pastor's or bishop's, etc. We *have to* follow Jesus completely and not be led astray by false prophets.

There are steps necessary to take in order to become a member of Christ's Church. You must believe (John 3:16); you must confess (Romans 10:9); you must repent (Acts 2:38); you must be baptized (Act 2:38); and you must have the works in addition to your faith (James 2:24). Once you become a faithful member of Christ's Church, He will hear your every request. You must die for Him in your sins and give Him your life (Matthew 16:25). The Lord patiently waits for all to come to Him, no matter how long it takes. Once your journey with the Lord begins, wait on Him as He waited on you and you will be astonished by His faithfulness in giving you what you have asked for. A person can promise you all you want, but the Lord's word is the *only* word that can be trusted.

One more quick note and I honestly hope this is not a shock to anyone that reads it. Like Jesus says, ask and you shall receive. This applies to many things—guidance in your life, being led to a new job, strength to let go of a person that you love that has hurt you deeply, a way to care for your children. Ask God anything that does not pertain to the world and He will lead you to that blessing at some point when He feels you are ready to receive it. Asking for worldly things, such as winning the lottery or for your favorite Super Bowl team to win, *is not* something God will give you. That is simply not how it works. God is not a genie from a magic lamp nor is He a fairy godmother. He does not *grant wishes*. He provides to us what we *need* and what He feels will help us in our lives. I hope that doesn't discourage you from following our great and mighty Lord. Remember, it is the devil that is of the world, not our God.

Being patient takes patience! What did I say in the very first chapter? God delivers in *His* time. You may receive your miracle overnight or it could very well take many days, months, or years. God does not promise to give you what you ask for just to say it. He means every word He says. Trust in the Lord and be patient with His plan as He has had patience with you for your entire life. Just remember…good things come to those who wait.

Kindness

"She opens her mouth in wisdom, and the teaching of kindness is on her tongue" (Proverbs 31:26).

Quit Hatin'

So I posted this post on Facebook the other day: "So if you hate haters, does that make you a hater?" Timmy responded with one word, "Yup." And he's right because we should love our enemies, remember? And, oh yeah, treat others as we want to be treated. As Christians, we need to take the word *hate* out of our vocabulary altogether. While we're talking about Facebook, I also want to mention an email that my boss sent to all of us girls working at the tanning salon. One of the salons got robbed yesterday (in the middle of the day!) and several ex-employees got word of it. They then posted some pretty nasty posts on the salon's page. My boss then said some *positive* words regarding these comments. She said, "I just want to say that if you see posts like that, just screenshot it to me so that I can handle it. Please do not get involved with it. Do not go to battle. Don't feed into it via Facebook or Twitter. I want you to take the high road." Did she read the revenge section of my book? I just thought that was so awesome of her!

Kindness can be kind of hard at times—when someone is rude to us, when we're cranky, when someone drives us flipping crazy, when someone hates on us. Whatever the case, it can be a challenge to be sweet in return. We have all been there, so why is it *so hard?* I honestly don't know; it just is! I saw a picture of this tattoo in a magazine with two guns crisscrossed accompanied by the phrase "Kill 'em with kindness." I *love* that phrase! But in the heat of a moment, it's an easy phrase to forget. Remember in the *love* section how I mentioned me and my brother were arguing and I finally texted him with an "I love you" (after he rudely said "I hate you")? That's a perfect example of killing 'em with kindness. It's almost like people are shocked when you are kind to them while they're being mean. It actually may really tick them off, but that is their own issue. As long as we do our part, that is all that matters. You never know, it just may encourage them to do the same in their next dispute with you (or someone else).

Another way we can be kind to others is by doing random acts of kindness. This goes along with the list I mentioned in the *Love Your Neighbor* section. My dad just bought me some super delicious donuts with frosting and sprinkles (that I am totally indulging in as we speak!). That was a much appreciated random act of kindness from him (Thank you, Daddy!). I often send cards to people in my family or to people from church. Sometimes I don't even know the church members if they are shut-ins (unable to physically go to services due to health issues), but that does not even matter to me. If a card cheers a person up, then that is just awesome! The smallest gesture, even just a smile, can be a *huge* act of kindness.

Whatever our acts of kindness consist of, we need to keep in mind that some people may not acknowledge them or give us the credit we may feel is due. Doing kind things should *not* be for the credit we think we deserve to receive. That is kind of a selfish act of kindness, don't you think? I am so guilty of that, too. Sometimes I will go to church and have a conversation with the person I sent a card to and they don't even say "Thank you." Or I will be driving and will let someone get in front of me and expect a thank-you wave, like, "Umm, hello! Where's my thank-you wave?!" This seriously happens to me on almost a daily basis. *Totally have to work on that, B!* Do you get my point, though? We should be kind just to be kind. No thank-yous necessary.

Lastly, where my haters at? Okay, I will include myself in this one because I am totally a hater at times. We have to start asking ourselves this question *before* we start hatin': Do we like being hated on? I know I sure don't! And hatin' isn't just something we do to the people we know personally. We can subconsciously hate on those who have more than us, such as seeing our dream car being driven; seeing someone that has more money than us; seeing someone prettier or more attractive or more in shape than us. Jealousy is a form of hate. We have to get past those feelings and stop hatin' on others for having the things we want or don't have.

> "Hatred stirs up strife, but love covers all transgressions" (Proverbs 10:12).

And as far as being hated on, I guess that's just something we're going to have to learn to accept. Sucks, right? That's so hard for me to accept because I am so well-mannered (thanks to my dad), and I am an extremely friendly person, so I think, *How can anyone not like me?* Lol. Not being conceited there, but, honestly, I don't get it sometimes. Like this one time at Target, I was in line to check out. There was a girl in front of me conversing with the cashier. There was smiling and laughing going on, so I assume it was friendly chatter. She leaves, and I'm up next. Do you know what the cashier chick did to me? She pretty much shunned me, even after I enthusiastically greeted her. Okay? This is stupid, but I was so upset about it I actually cried when I got to my car. Like my auntie said to me, "Not everyone is going to or has to like you, B." The hardest part is not stooping to their level in the midst of a hater moment. It'll be okay…

Goodness

"And He said, "I Myself will make all My goodness pass before you, and will proclaim the name of the Lord before you; and I will be gracious to whom I will be gracious, and will show compassion on whom I will show compassion" (Exodus 33:19).

In my NASV concordance, *goodness* is defined as "excellence, value." To do good unto others may be challenging, especially to those who have wronged you; more so to those who have wronged you over and over again. I, myself, believe I possess a wealth of goodness in me (or at least in my deeds). Perhaps the greatest example of goodness I have come to show in my life is toward a boy that I love very deeply. He has done me wrong countless times (we're talking in the hundreds), yet I am still kind and generous to him. If I told you all that he has done to me, you would surely curse me for my goodness toward him. I often wonder if it is the Lord in me that acts that way toward him or if it is the devil in him that charms it out of me. Either way, this quality I possess (most of the time) is one that our Lord wants us all to have. And I know that if I can be this good to a boy who has wreaked havoc in my head and in my heart, then we are all capable of being good to anyone that crosses our paths. Allow me to share with you the goodness I have shown...

Let's call this boy *Shane*. I met Shane at an NA meeting. For those of you that do not know what that means, it stands for *Narcotics Anonymous*. I chose to go to these meetings when I was pregnant with my son, Chase, and decided to establish a new group of sober friends. I randomly chose a meeting place by doing a Google search online. When I arrived, there was Shane. He approached me, and I honestly had no interest in him. To make a long, long story short, I gave Shane my number upon his request and started something with him that has brought me to a very dark place. We will have been together for almost a year now. And I say *together* because I still am allowing him in my life (for only God truly knows why). From the first few weeks of getting to know Shane, I fell in love. As did he. I knew it wasn't a good idea from the events that took place not even a month after knowing him. His ex-girlfriend of eighteen years called my cell phone and said a whole lot of stuff about him that I knew deep down I should not involve myself with. I chose to disregard the ex and continued to pursue Shane. Since then, our relationship is all but normal. He has mentally and emotionally abused me every day. He has ditched me every week. He has broken countless promises. He has cursed me, belittled me, threatened me, insulted me, degraded me, stolen from me, abandoned me, lied to me, cheated on me (supposedly), horrified me. I like how one of my best girlfriends has put it—he has *destroyed* me. And I am not perfect in my goodness toward him but I have certainly treated him better than he deserves. When he calls me names, I call them back. When he's stolen from me, I have reported him to the police. This boy has taken and manipulated me to spend over $20,000 on him in less than one year. I received a big chunk of money last year and he needed help after he had already been a horrible person to me—left me alone on the first night we moved in together when I was pregnant in not such a good neighborhood; stole my car in the middle of the night along with money out of my purse; slept over at his ex's house numerous times. That's just to name a few. I still helped him out when he asked. By the way, did I mention he's a drug addict? I hate drugs. Drugs are not only bad for us physically, mentally, emotionally, and spiritually; they are a sad excuse to avoid reality and the plans God has for us. Anyways, all of the money Shane manipulated me to spend was to feed his habit. Shane was homeless since I met him and needed a place to stay. I bought not one but *two* apartments for him, trusting that he was going to help me out since I helped him out. What did he do? He never paid me rent and cost me $5,750 alone in rent just to live in two different apartments for less than three months. All I do is try to help him beat his habit.

Want to hear some worse stuff he's done? The night of my delivery of my son, he stole my car for five hours. Mind you, Shane had been dating me since I was ten weeks pregnant. He often mentioned how excited he was to be there for me in the hospital. Want to hear something worse? The very next night, he stole my car for sixteen hours. He had relapsed. He not only stole my car but my cell phone as well. There I was, almost five months ago, all alone in my hospital room with my newborn with no cell phone and no car and no supportive, loving boyfriend like he promised. All for a stupid drug. You think that would have pushed me to the point of saying "Screw this, I'm done!" Sadly, it didn't. Since then, he has manipulated me even more and mentally abused me to the point of suicidal thoughts. I was suicidal before I met him because I lost a boyfriend to a suicidal overdose just eight months before meeting Shane. Everything got better for me when I found out I was pregnant. I overcame that darkness and accepted my loss and moved on peacefully. Shane has completely taken me back to that place of horror. For one, he threatens me that *he* is going to kill *himself* if I leave him. He knows I lost that boy and uses that against me. So awful! I can't handle that. I knew a girl that lost two boyfriends in her life to suicide and I always told her story and said that if that ever happened to me, I wouldn't be able to go on. You know what Shane did to me about a month ago? He filled up a syringe with water and told me it was bleach and said that he was going to kill himself with it (inject it into his veins) if I didn't give him money for drugs. I believed him until he mentioned the money part. I knew it was just another manipulation, but who does that to someone they love? My main point in sharing this with you—I have always been good to him after all of these horrible things he has done to me. I have *still* bought him things he's asked for. I have *still* allowed him to spend the night when he has nowhere to go and it's 17 degrees out. Remember in the *Show Some Love* section about showing love to everyone, no matter what? Talk about hard!

And one more thing… Let me tell you yet *another* example of my excellence and value. Shane just called me (April 15, 2016, 11:20 a.m.) and told me how mad he is at *me* for the charges I put on him from stealing *from me* and I still had the decency to apologize to him, even though it is purely *his* fault for doing that stuff to me in the first place! Don't ever let anyone take the goodness from you no matter what they do to you because in the end we are all judged for our actions. Yes, maybe I took things a little too far in reporting him to the police but I cannot take it back, just like he cannot take back all the things he has done to me. Let your excellence reflect in everything you do and you will be rewarded by our kind and loving Lord. I pray for Shane ten times a day, asking the Lord to rescue him from the devil and to give him the desire to serve the Lord and do good unto others. One day he will be reading this book from a jail cell knowing this is all about him and that he caused me a world of pain and I only hope he truly feels remorse for everything he has done to me.

Let's look at some examples in the Bible of how Christ and his disciples showed their goodness.

The story of Jonah. I love this story. There are two points of greatness in this short yet amazing book. I encourage you to read it! Most of us learned about Jonah in Bible school as children. He was the man that got swallowed by a great, giant fish. God gave Jonah a duty to fulfill. He was to go to the great city of Nineveh to warn the people there of their wickedness (Jonah 1:2). Jonah had a fear of doing this, so he jumped ship with a crew of men to Tarshish to flee from the presence of the Lord (Jonah 1:3). We all know that we cannot hide from the Lord, including Jonah, and this disobedience angered the Lord. A great storm came upon the ship, and Jonah confessed to the men that it was because of him (Jonah 1:4–14). The men tossed Jonah into the sea and the sea became calm (Jonah 1:15). God appointed a big fish to swallow Jonah, and he was in the stomach of the fish for three days and three nights (Jonah 1:17). Jonah prayed (Jonah 2:1–9). The Lord heard Jonah's prayer and commanded the fish to spit him out (Jonah 2:10). So the Lord commanded Jonah, again, to go to the city of Nineveh to warn them of their evil deeds and what will happen if they do not stop (Jonah 3:1–4). The people of Nineveh heard Jonah and believed in God (Jonah 3:5). The city declared a fast and took action to cover themselves and pray on their wickedness that they might each be forgiven so that the city is not destroyed (Jonah 3:5–9). In verse 10, when God saw their deeds and that they turned from their wicked ways, God declared He would *not* destroy the city as He planned. That is the first point in the Lord's goodness. He gave the city a warning. They took it seriously. God gave them a second chance. How great our God is! As the story continues, Jonah becomes angry that God had compassion on Nineveh, an enemy of Israel. He wanted God's goodness to be shown only to Israelites, not the Gentiles (Jonah 4:1). Jonah felt that God should not have granted His forgiveness to the city. What Jonah didn't comprehend was that it was not his place to be angry and he had no reason for such anger towards God. Jonah then goes out and makes a shelter for himself. God grew a plant for Jonah to give him shade and comfort from the hot, beating sun (Jonah 4:5–6). The Lord then destroys the plant. God then gives Jonah a reason to be angry when He kills the plant that *He* grew over Jonah to give him shade and comfort (Jonah 4:5–9). In verse 11, God says, "Should I not have compassion on Nineveh, the great city in which there are more than 120,000 persons who do not know *the difference* between their right and left hand, as well as many animals?" Verse 11 points out the second act of goodness of our Lord. He made Jonah realize that He is good to those that obey Him and that it is *only* His decision to show or not show compassion to those that repent. It does not matter how others feel about someone or something. God cares about each and every one of us individually. He is such a compassionate God and He is awesome.

Another example of goodness in the Bible is the story of Rahab. It begins in the second chapter of Joshua in the Old Testament. Joshua secretly sent two men as spies out to view the land of Jericho. The men set out and came upon the house of Rahab where they stayed (Joshua 2:1–2). The king of Jericho had told Rahab to bring the spies to him, but Rahab told the king that the men came to her but she did not know where they went (Joshua 2:3–4). That was clearly a lie. Rahab continued to tell the king that the men went out and that he had better pursue them, while in the meantime she had hid them on the roof of her home (Joshua 2:5–6). Rahab confronted the men, telling them she is aware that the land is theirs. She kindly asked the men to deliver her mother, father, brothers and sisters, all from death (Joshua 2:9–13). The men agreed to this and swore on an oath to keep their promise since she kept them safe and did not turn them over to be killed (Joshua 2:14). The story continues, but we will stop there. Rahab was exceedingly good to these men. She could have easily had them pursued and killed, but she chose to do good over evil. In exchange for her goodness, the spies also were good to her in keeping their word.

Lastly, and as always, Jesus commits so many acts of goodness throughout His *entire* life. Even before Jesus was born, God delivered a message through an angel to Joseph, the husband of Mary, who was the mother of Jesus, to tell of the greatness of this child. The angel said to Joseph, "Do not be afraid to take Mary as your wife; for the child who has been conceived in her is of the Holy Spirit" (Matthew 1:20). In verse 21, the angel goes on to say, "She will bear a Son; and you shall call His name Jesus, for He will save His people from their sins." It is hard to understand God, Jesus, and the Holy Spirit. It took me a long time to comprehend it, but they are all one. When I say Jesus is great, I am actually inferring all *three* of these as great. Jesus is God in the human form. Read Matthew 1:23, *"Behold, the virgin shall be with child and shall bear a Son, and they shall call His name Emmanuel"* which, translated, means "God with us." Therefore, God is good. Jesus is good. The Holy Spirit is good. Jesus gave the blind sight, allowed the lame to walk, cleansed the lepers, caused the deaf to hear, raised the dead, and preached to the poor (Matthew 11:5). Until His death on the cross, even Jesus forgave and accepted the criminal that was crucified with Him. "And He said to him, 'Truly I say to you, today you shall be with Me in Paradise'" (Luke 23:43). Every act of Jesus was of goodness, and to this day *is* goodness.

Oh, yeah. Let me mention one more thing about my personal goodness. On this very night—April 15, 2016—the same day that Shane called me and yelled at me for reporting him to the police, would you believe he asked me to get him some food? You know what I said to him? "Sure, what do you want?" I literally went to McDonald's and bought him a value meal and large vanilla milkshake per his request. Yes, the same boy that has taken thousands of dollars from me, stolen my car the night I gave birth, and threatened to kill himself in front of me with a fake syringe of *bleach* if I didn't give him money. So why did I get him food? Because I choose to see the good in people, no matter how evil they are or may have been. That's just the goodness in me. I hate myself for it, but I know the Lord is well pleased. April 16, 3:30 p.m. Bought him $60 of groceries. April 17: bought him an outfit and food to have a picnic.

I have to give it to Shane, though. For as much wrong that I have done to him—three charges; packed up his stuff and moved us out of our first apartment (where I just moved back home and left him homeless. I left him fresh folded laundry and food, of course.); gave him a black eye and fat lip; blocked him numerous times; cancelled the cell phone I gave him; threatened to call the cops; kicked him out of my car; drove off and left him; smacked him in the face; threw his stuff in the street; kicked him out of our second apartment; ripped up his very first drawings for me; set him up to have his ex-girlfriend pull up on us in the street where she got out of the car and hit him; called him horrible names; and a lot more. Do you know after all that stuff (that I really only did because he made me crazy), he *still* forgives me and says he loves me and wants to marry me? He does, and I totally give him credit for that. He truly brings out this evil person in me, and I hope he knows I admit that 100 percent. But, in a way, I have done a lot of that stuff to him (or most of it, actually) so that he *will hate me*. Would you believe that he doesn't hate me at all? I know he loves me and I love him to death. And for him to still love me after all of that? I have to admit, there's a lot of goodness in him, too. That's why I love him so much and always will. God gave me him to love. It's unfortunate that Shane cannot count my goodness as his nor can I force him to possess it. That is totally his choice; I cannot force it. I so wish I could, but I have tried and tried and tried and it just does not work. I remember reading in the book *The Secret* that you cannot visualize for someone else. Only you have the ability to visualize for yourself and fulfill your own journey. But I am not giving up just yet. My goodness for him will always be there because that's just who I am. Christ is that way, and I want to follow in His footsteps. I love you, Shane. Thank you for always having a desire to be good to me. Please keep trying and pray to the Lord above that He will guide your way. You can do it babe. Thank you for our picnic in the park today. I love you.

May 7, 2016: twenty-three days sober down the drain. I wake up to a frantic call from Shane's stepdad asking me if Shane came home with me last night when I left their house. My stomach immediately dropped as my fear of him relapsing once again came true. I called him eighty-one times. No answer. How hard is it to show true goodness in a stressful situation like this? Nearly impossible (for me). I texted mean, hateful things and even suspended his brand-new cell phone account (He literally bought it the night before). I did have some goodness in that I only wanted to make it harder for him to obtain drugs (that's my twisted justification of it, anyway). But my actions were not examples that we are to show to one another. Jesus never took action against anyone who insulted Him, threatened Him, beat him, or killed Him (all found in Matthew 27). He is our true example of that goodness we *must* possess. And, I must say, it doesn't feel very good after committing acts of unkindness toward others. Rather, it leaves (me) feeling guilty, ashamed, embarrassed, and downright evil. I am truly sorry to this boy for all of my hateful reactions, for not controlling my anger, and for letting the devil get the best of me. I might as well have been the drug addict and/or thief that he was because a sin is a sin is a sin. No goodness is no goodness, period. May I learn from this relationship to always show the goodness in my character (like Jesus did) no matter what. If you struggle with this, pray upon it and request to let the goodness that Jesus possessed to flow through your veins so that you may bleed goodness in every act you commit. I will pray for yours and ask that you pray for mine.

I will close with this. As horrible as all of the things Shane has done to me, he did an amazing (yet heartbreaking) thing today. Well, I told him we were over. That I could not have him in my life anymore, even though he's all I want (when he's sober). He's all I love and is the second boy I have lost to drugs in my life. So what did he do? After putting up with his behavior for just over a year now, he told me I need to stop chasing him because I deserve better. He is right. I love him more than anything and my heart is in pieces right now as I write this sad ending to our story that I didn't want to write. I wanted to tell you that me and him are happily together, that he is drug-free, that he loves me unconditionally, that we have a beautiful baby girl together. We won't have any of those things, and it hurts so bad I honestly do not know if I will ever get over him. He will always hold a special place in my heart. He truly had the best of intentions throughout our relationship but failed to overcome evil with good. I will always remember all of our good times. Tonight, Shane is homeless, roaming the streets, and stealing from stores to get drug money. I know he doesn't want to be that way, but he is sadly without God in his life and blames the Lord for the hand he was dealt with—his addiction. If goodness comes from the Lord, then what comes from the devil? Only evil. I pray Shane understands that one day and overcomes all of his badness with goodness. Goodnight, Shane. I love you forever.

Acting good is a choice. We all have the choice to act good or bad, even Jesus had to make that choice on a daily basis. Countless examples in the Bible reflect goodness and badness, but those that chose goodness reaped great reward. Be good in *everything* you do, even if it kills you. For it is better to die with an act of goodness than an act of badness because once we die we can no longer ask for forgiveness for our acts of badness. Let God know of your good and He shall repay you (all of us) greatly.

Tiger Stripes

A tiger is my favorite animal. To me, these animals have the most outward beauty in all species on this earth. Each tiger is unique in its stripes in that no one tiger is *ever* alike. Each stripe is different on every tiger that exists. And just a fun fact to know—a tiger's skin is striped just as the fur represents! Anyways, I have a tiger tattoo with the words *My Disguise* written underneath it. In my pastime, a few friends and I would *animalize* people; that is, compare a person to an animal according to their personality and looks. I have always compared myself to a tiger for two reasons. For one, a tiger is extremely beautiful on the outside. Not from a conceited standpoint, but I am absolutely blessed with an outward beauty. Reason number two, and this isn't necessarily a good thing, I possess a fierceness on the inside, if you will, like that of a tiger. No matter how beautiful a tiger may be, and it *always* is, a tiger's main goal in life is to hunt for food. Have you ever watched how tigers attack their prey in the wild? I have watched it many times on television. It is extremely hard for me to watch. How can such a beautiful animal turn so vicious? It almost appears downright evil. However, animals live by instinct and their instinct is to survive no matter what they do to get their food. I usually cry every time I see a poor antelope brutally attacked and eaten to their demise by a predator. It truly breaks my heart. But as my dad always says to me, it's *part of nature.*

As for humans, we were created differently. God did not create us to attack one another in a brutal way. He did not create us to attack each other, period. He created us to love one another and to love Him. He gave us *all* tiger stripes, meaning He gave us all an outward beauty to possess, no matter what we feel on the inside. He did not create the evil that can be in us—that is Satan—He only created things of love. Satan wants us to show our fierceness on the outside as much as possible. It is Satan's goal to win each and every one of us over before the Lord returns to us here on Earth. He wants to take as many souls to hell with him that he can because he does not care about our final destinations. He only cares about taking that which is good away from God. One of my favorite verses regarding Satan and his evilness is found in 1 Peter 5:8. It says, "Be of sober *spirit*, be on the alert. Your adversary, the devil, prowls around like a roaring lion, seeking someone to devour." Satan disguises himself as anything and everything to take our inner and outer beauty and turn us against God. We need to resist him and not allow any of our urges of evil within us to break free of that outer beauty that we all, like tigers, possess. *No matter what!* Yes, it is *extremely* hard! And I, for one, am *constantly* working on this! Satan gets me *all the time!* But I am determined to beat him with beauty. I am made *of God.* I was brought into this world *by God.* And I am only going to *serve God.* I will wear my stripes proudly every day, as the beautiful tigers and tigresses do in the wild. We are all beautiful creatures and we need to resist the devil in every attempt he makes to cause us to be angry, deceitful, hateful, ugly, and—my sister-in-law's favorite word—*icky*. A tiger is strong and beautiful and confident. May we all learn to disguise ourselves as tigers *every single day.*

Faithfulness

"The righteous man shall live by faith" (Galatians 3:11).

According to the order of this book, this appears to be the seventh chapter. For me, it is my final chapter. I tend to write my chapters in the order that I struggle with them, and I struggled with my faith chapter (in my life) for a long, long time. I have had so many doubts in my life. I have also had so many miracles! So, deep down, I know that having faith is *the secret* to an amazing life. We are all tested in our faith throughout our lives with the different obstacles we go through. It is up to us to decide if we will give up, give in, or have the faith we need to conquer our demons and win our battles. Every one of us has a unique story. Each of us has been through something awful in our lives. As time passes, we overcome those once awful things and stumble upon something else that seems even worse. We are constantly battling the devil, fighting to stay alive in a world that seems so chaotic in this new day of age. We *must* rely on God to get us through our toughest battles. If we rely on ourselves, the outcomes we reach are not of the greatest possible potential destined to each and every one of us. God *promises* with faith we will be rewarded *greatly!* We must learn to trust Him, and when I say *we,* I am especially saying *me!*

My faith has walked on broken glass in several instances in my life, the biggest involving breakups. My overly dramatic sadness (though I am diagnosed with depression) caused me to question my faith with a couple of boys, two in particular—J and Shane. Both of these boys were drug addicts that only my future self discovered shortly after falling for them (I was never exposed to hard drugs, so I did not know the signs). Once I was attached to them, I had trouble leaving them despite their horrible habits that came with constant lies, mind games, and heartache. Both of these boys have a different story with a very different outcome. With J, I honestly stayed with him because I was so physically attracted to him. He had nothing to offer me, and when I say nothing, I mean *nothing!* I moved in with him shortly after I met him in a house that was anything but up to my standards—a poor house in Cleveland. His drug habit soon cost us *all* of our utilities to be shut off. I was peeing in the backyard on a daily basis, using candles to see at night, resorting to hand sanitizer because we had no water to use soap. My life was *miserable,* yet I stayed. Why? Would you believe that I feared I would be sad about this boy forever? I lacked the faith to trust and believe that everything would be okay in the future. I recognize now that my faith was weak and I trusted only myself that maybe if I stayed with J he could overcome his addiction and we could be the happy couple I wanted us to be. My faith wasn't completely weak, however, because I did pack up and leave. Twice! I moved *all* of my stuff out of the house two separate times, trying my absolute hardest to believe God would cure my tears and pain and anxiety of the life I was living just for a boy I loved. Although going back and staying with J was not the wisest decision I have made, God soon took J from me a few short months later from a suicidal overdose, so I then had no choice but to choose to have faith that everything would be okay without him. Moving on without J seemed impossible and my faith was completely empty for about seven months. In the end, I became pregnant with my son Chase, and of all of the days I found out about this angel inside of me, it was on the day that would have been the first year anniversary for me and J. And, no, the baby was not J's, but I do believe I was given a boy to fill that void of missing J forever because all along I thought it was a *girl!* God works in magical ways if we have faith, and I truly believe that this example is one of my most treasured (although heartbreaking) miracles of my life. Thank you, Lord, for pulling me through!

    The second boy, Shane, is *still* the love of my life. He is *still* my boyfriend, even while he is in rehab as we speak. The difference between Shane and J is that Shane has *the world* to offer me if he chooses to let his habit go. He is *so* talented in every way a man can be talented. He can build stuff, fix things, draw, dance, make me laugh, encourage me, comfort me, love me, and so much more. He has three beautiful children and can be an amazing father when he is straight. He is so beyond perfect that I cannot, for the life of me, leave him behind. After everything I mentioned about him in the last chapter, you would surely hope I move on from him, right? I mean, my family *hates* him (which is very un-Christianlike of them, just saying), and his family really doesn't care for me much, either, since I did report him to the police and caused him to stay in county jail not once but twice. Through *everything* we have been through, I want this man a part of my life forever. Believe me, I have *tried* to let him go. I have *prayed* to God hundreds, even thousands, of times to increase my faith to know that I am better off without him. But just like J and even a million times more, I fear I will never fall out of love with Shane. That scares the heck out of me! Then I thought about my love for Shane. Why is it *so* impossible to let this guy go? Why do I fear missing and loving him forever? Why do I feel the need to keep trying with him, to try to help him overcome his weakness in his life? Then it dawned on me. Perseverance! The most crucial element that makes up our faith is *perseverance*. The very definition of the word *perseverance* is "persistence." Persistence is *never giving up!* Your faith is *not* weak if you persevere. *My* faith was not weak with these boys, and it is *not* weak with Shane. I am a nurturer and a comforter and a forgiver. I am a spiritual teacher. My very purpose in life is to help, encourage, and save others. How can I save someone if I am so quick to give up? I can't! I *have faith* in my perseverance. I *have faith* that I am doing the very thing God wants me to be doing at this very moment in my life. Does it seem crazy to others? Absolutely! My family and friends would *never* take the chances I have taken with this boy. God has purposed me to save people from the devil before His Son returns to judge the earth. If that includes a boy that has wronged me in the past, then so be it. I read an amazing quote on Pinterest just yesterday that says, "None of us should be defined by the worst thing we've ever done" (Kevin R. Duncan). How true is that quote? It is so easy to point out everyone else's mistakes and even easier to forever judge them based on one completely awful thing that they have done. I have always made it a point in my life to forgive the mistakes others have made, especially toward me. Like it is said in the Bible, how can we be forgiven of our sins if we do not forgive others (Matthew 6:14)? Shane deserves my forgiveness and he deserves a fulfilling life just like the rest of us. God wants us all to live a happy, content life with Him. Shane and I have yet to face our toughest battle—being apart from each other. We have agreed to take that leap of faith once he is released from rehab to part ways so each of us can focus on our lives and taking care of the business we need to take care of as responsible adults. Not only that, but we each need to grow in our faith and living for God. There are many parts of my personality that require me to change in order for Shane and I to be together. My trust for him was broken many times and as a result of that I am quick to anger, resentment, and judgement. We cannot and will not be happy if we live in the past. I need to put aside *all* of the past, as does he. As far as our relationship and faith, I have faith that God will strengthen us individually so that we can (if it is God's will) be together one day, stronger than imaginable. If something goes wrong in our relationship again, then I have faith that God wanted me to learn yet *another* lesson that will without a doubt increase my faith even more.

While I struggle with my faith and question if me and Shane will really end up together, I do not put my faith in *him*. Faith should *never* be put in a man (or woman); only God. This is why it displeases God greatly to be a part of a *denomination*. A denomination is a manmade religion. It may contain some truths of the Word, but *men* have contributed their own interpretations or opinions of what *they* believe so that it conveniences them. I have faith that God will bring me to the future He wants me to have. If that is with Shane, then that would be awesome. If it is not, then I have faith that God will bring each of us through our heartbreaks and struggles to a better outcome than we thought possible. Have faith in the Lord and He will see you through your hardships.

As humans, we all have doubts and we all have fears. The fear of change is probably the most feared fear among us. It suggests discomfort, stress, anxiety, anger, frustration, sadness. So basically, change is freaking hard! It requires courage, strength, and perseverance. I believe change can be so hard for people that it is the very reason they stay in their same situations, whether that be remaining an addict, staying in an abusive relationship, working a job that you absolutely hate, among others. Change is scary, but God and His disciples have mentioned its rewards through *faith* in the Bible countless times. Correction...faith *and* works. "You see that a man is justified by works and not by faith alone" (James 2:24). If there is one example for us to turn to in the Bible when our faith is weak, let us all look to the book of Job. If any of us thinks we have been through a lot or we have had it harder than others, please read the book of Job. This man endured more than it seems possible, certainly worse than any of us have ever experienced, yet he remained faithful to the Lord. The book of Job contains forty-two chapters and I finally read them all at once! I used a study Bible to help me, although we must be careful with those Bibles as they are interpreted by man and *not* by God. My intentions were to go through and break down all of those chapters for you. But after doing that to the first eight chapters, I decided my confidence in interpreting some of the parts of Job were just too hard for me. I do not want to be responsible for saying the wrong thing, so I will leave it up to you to study it on your own or with a preacher. Just know this about Job—Job feared the Lord and remained strong in his faith, even when his children and possessions were taken from him. He did not allow the devil to convince him to go against God, and that, my friends, is the greatest challenge of all in this cold, cruel world.

Two lessons of faith come from the book of Job. The acts of faith of Job is a given. He does not curse God once, despite his unfortunate circumstances. The second lesson, and perhaps the first act of faith of the book that may go unnoticed, is the faith that the Lord has in Job. God knows the man He created Job to be and trusted His instincts that Job would not curse Him despite what the devil may do to tempt him to do that. God believed and did not hesitate to allow Satan to do with Job what he wanted to do. Our God has faith in all of us to make the right choices in life, even when it seems hopeless, for when one gets to the point of no hope, that is when most of us look to God and ask Him for His help. I encourage everyone to *always* have faith in God, whether you are at a bad point in your life or a good point. Having faith prospers more and more faithful acts from our God. As the Lord says in my absolute favorite verse of the Bible, "Ask, and it will be given to you; seek, and you will find; knock, and it will be opened to you" (Matthew 7:7). Ask… Receive… Believe!

Another lesson of faith in the Bible is demonstrated by Abraham in the very beginning of the Old Testament. Actually, there are two lessons within this story. While I read all of it as I did the book of Job, I am not going to break it down for you. I do encourage you to read about Abraham and his family beginning in Genesis chapter 17. The very first lesson of faith taught is in regard to Abraham's wife Sarah who was told by God that she would bear a son at the age of ninety-nine. Sarah laughed at this and did not have any faith that it was possible. In Genesis 21, Isaac is born. The second lesson of faith is about Abraham and his son, Isaac. God commanded Abraham to offer up Isaac, his *only* son whom he loved very much, as a burnt offering (Genesis 22:2). The usual thing to offer as a sacrifice was an animal, but God was testing Abraham's faith and insisted he literally burn his son on the stake. Not once did Abraham question God or hesitate to follow His command. When Abraham and Isaac got to the place God had commanded him to do this, Abraham built an altar and bound his son on it with the wood underneath with a knife in his hand to slay his son (Genesis 22:9–10). As Abraham stretched out his hand to slay Isaac, the angel of the Lord called to him and said, "Do not stretch out your hand against the lad, and do nothing to him; for now I know that you fear God, since you have not withheld your son, your only son, from Me" (Genesis 22:12). I just want to say real quick that I have a son, Chase, my angel that literally saved my life, and I *cannot imagine* if God had commanded me to kill him! The faith that Abraham possessed is just so unreal to me, I am just stunned at this amazing act of faith! To fear the Lord so much and have that much faith that if he did not obey God's command that God would punish him… I am just blown away. Would you sacrifice your only child? Think about how hard that would be. *Really* dwell on it for a second. That is asking the impossible, don't you think? So hear this. If you *ever* think that you can't do something or that you can't overcome something that you are struggling with, just remember that if Abraham had the strength and faith to tie his son to an altar to kill and sacrifice him to God, you can do *anything!* That is why we have examples of faith in the Bible to know that absolutely anything is possible with the Lord. So I beg you now, if you are down and hopeless and faithless, *please* get on your knees right now and ask God for the strength and courage that Abraham had in order to overcome whatever it is that you are struggling with. I know my faith just increased tenfold!

While walking in the Metroparks today, I found myself thinking a lot about my future: where will I end up? Who will I be with? Where will my path lead me? As my mind wondered in an abundance of questions, I came to a crossroads (literally). I looked up at the street signs where I was about to cross and there were two roads to choose from—*Valley Parkway* and *Shepherd Lane*. This was *way* too big of a coincidence to ignore as I pondered the outcomes of my future. It was as if God was speaking *right to me*. When I thought about these two roads, two thoughts immediately came to me. When I thought of *Valley Parkway*, I instantly thought about the verse in the Bible that says, "Even though I walk through the valley of the shadow of death" (Psalm 23:4). For *Shepherd Lane,* I thought of the verse, "The Lord is my Shepherd, I shall not want" (Psalm 23:1). In that very moment, the Lord was showing me that there is only one of two paths that I can choose. I can choose destruction and walk in the darkness (with the devil) or I can choose Him (my Shepherd) and never be led astray. I stayed on *Valley Parkway* because *Shepherd Lane* leads to the Nature Center lol. But I knew in my heart that as long as I continue on a path of righteousness, then no matter where I end up and who I end up with, my future will undoubtedly be perfect. That was such a neat way for the Lord to speak to me. If you find yourself at a crossroads in your life, I pray you take the path that leads to life. Life is hard. *Believe me,* I know this, and being a Christian in this cruel world is even harder, but the few who find this path and take it will not be let down by our loving and faithful Lord.

One last example I have for you was something that just happened to me recently. It was a small thing to happen, but when I really thought about it, it turned out to be a lesson relating to faith and how we possess it. I was giving my son a bath and he became fascinated with the shower curtain. He tugged on it quite a few times, and by the end of his bath, the whole curtain came down. I got him out of the bath, dried him off, got him dressed, then returned to the bathroom, like, *Okay, I better fix this.* The funny thing is, the bar to my shower curtain had been on *backwards,* so every time I attempted to pull it, it would get caught on the bar and I would have to fight it to get the curtain to the end. Every single time I had gotten in the shower since I moved into this house, I would tell myself, "I really need to switch this bar around." Do you know how long I have lived here and have been saying that? I have lived here for a little over *four years!* The point—don't be lazy about your faith and don't put it off. There are many obstacles in our lives that we *can* and *will* overcome, if we put our faith in the Lord *every single day* and *every single moment.* Had I fixed my shower curtain years ago, I wouldn't have had such frustration every time I got into the shower. More than that, if we live by faith *now* and don't *wait till later* to believe in God and His great plans for each and every one of us, then we save a whole lot of wasted time before it's too late. We do not know when our last waking moments of our lives are going to be. We are not promised tomorrow, and if we are not right with the Lord, it *will* be too late to ask for forgiveness. God promises those that are faithful a reward of eternity with Him, which sounds a whole lot better than eternal darkness, wouldn't you agree? Act now, show some faith, believe that God will bring you through whatever it is that you are going through, and you will be rewarded greatly! Remember this one final thing—God is at work for you and for me in every experience we have (good *or* bad), and we need to *trust* Him that He knows what He is doing and that everything will work out for the best. Turn to God and He will turn to you!

In closing, I would like to announce some very great news on this beautiful fall day. First of all, if it is not obvious, this chapter was written over a number of months (four, to be exact) and my circumstances have changed dramatically for the better and I want to say I owe it *all* to my faith! Okay, to start off, Shane and I are happily together. Two weeks ago, Shane completed treatment at a rehab facility. On no influence of mine, he decided it would be best for him to further his sobriety and stay in a three-quarter house (a sober living house for recovering addicts). The first morning he woke up there, on the day of his official fifth month of sobriety, he called me and told me something that meant the world to me. He said, "Babe, I just want to tell you that this is the happiest I have *ever* been in my life and I owe it all to you." Now that was so very sweet of Shane to thank me and give me the credit for that (I love you, babe!), but I praised the Lord as soon as I hung up and said, "Thank You, Lord. Thank You. Thank You. Thank You!" Shane and I both know that if it weren't for God, I would have never been that angel Shane needed to give him a little nudge to live a clean and sober life. And on November 11, 2016 (11-11), Shane and I found out that we are expecting a child! While I am overwhelmed with joy about this miraculous event, I know now more than ever that I need to have faith that everything will be alright. Currently, I live at my dad's with my almost-one-year-old son, Chase, and have not had a job in six months (since I got fired from the vet). My savings are almost entirely out and, by the way, my dad still does not approve of Shane so he will not even let him over the house. I am *terrified* to tell my dad and family (my mom, brother, and sister-in-law still disapprove, too) that I am pregnant *again,* as my son is only one year old and his father is not in his life at all. With that being said, I am praying my butt off that things will work out the way God has planned for me and my family. All I can do is pray and have faith that everything will be okay and that one day my family will accept Shane as the love of my life and welcome our child into their arms as they did for Chase. To me, my situation is super scary and at times I really don't know how things are going to work out, but then I think about this book I am writing and that God puts me in tough spots to demonstrate my faith to Him so that I can share my story with you and inspire you to have faith in your situation. Things can only get *better* with faith, not worse. Alright, here's to having faith in God no matter how crazy you think your circumstances are.

Are you guys ready for this curveball?

It is one month later that I found out I am pregnant with Shane's baby and I know the Lord has dropped this bomb on me to choose faith in *Him*, not Shane. Shane had six months clean on December 9, 2016. Shane relapsed December 9, 2016. He lied and said he went to work. He shut his phone off all day long, torturing my mind to assume that he was lying in a ditch dead on the side of the road. My reality has gone from fairy tale ending to worst nightmare ever. Shane finally called me on December 10, 2016, not remorseful in the least for what he had done to me and caused me to think. He asked me for a ride to pick up his stuff at his sober living house that he was kicked out of at 1:00 a.m. this morning. I agreed only because he owes me so much money I figured I would keep his stuff as ransom for him to pay me weekly. When I met him on the corner of the worst area in Cleveland aka the hood, I got out of my car to help him put my bike that he borrowed in my trunk. All of a sudden, his ex-girlfriend pulls up saying he was just at her house. My heart sank because I knew that was true. He called me from his phone an hour earlier and I heard kids in the background, so he probably pocket dialed me on accident, not to mention she lived two streets away from where we met. I don't know how many of you have ever been cheated on or told that you were being cheated on by an envious ex, but let me tell you I have been dealing with this girl for our entire relationship and it is just awful. To think the person who tells you he loves you to the moon and back and that he wants you to have his child and to marry you and be with you forever is cheating on you with the woman he left you for, that is just heart-wrenching. As the anger built up inside of me from hearing her say those words, I felt myself lose it. Shane and I then got into a physical altercation (yet again) and the cops were called. This time it was ugly and he got arrested…again. He has been arrested with me in his presence three times now. In the meantime, I went to the sober house to collect his belongings since he owes me around $30,000 now, so I decided to take his stuff. I heard Shane shout from the cop car, "Do not let that b**** take my stuff. Call my brother and he will come get it." Fortunately, Shane's brother hates when he gets high and not only refused to get his stuff but verbally stated and texted the owner of the sober living house to "Give everything to Brooke (me)." Now while I feel horribly guilty for sending him right back to jail, I did not feel guilty for taking his things because deep down I wanted him to call me and forgive me, like he always does, and me having his stuff would be a reason for him to do that. I got home after going to a girlfriend's house to get my mind off things and decided to go through some of Shane's things. To my complete and utter surprise, I found two things that shattered my heart and every memory we had created in that very instant. Shane had drawn two drawings that read this—*Shane & Tia 2016* with hearts and then an envelope that says *Tia*. Shane only draws when he is locked up. He was locked up six months ago. I am absolutely heartbroken and stunned that he has been playing me while he has been *sober*. It's unacceptable either way to cheat on someone. But when you date an addict, it is reasonable to assume it while he is high. For him to play me while he was locked up and drawing me the same pictures with *my* name on it and hearts and love and kisses forever is just the lowest blow I could ever feel. He made me feel so loved every single day, and now I just feel like it was all a lie. A lie for what, though? Like, what did he get out of doing that to me? Why did he do this to me? How could he do this to me? Why did I deserve this?

Well, you know what, guys? It *all* comes down to faith. Had I had the faith in God to trust Him that I would be okay if I left Shane two years ago, then maybe this wouldn't have happened. Of course, this wouldn't have happened! But was it *supposed* to happen? Yes. Absolutely. *This* is my moment of faith. This is where I draw the line between Shane (man) and God. *This* is where I find my strength! *This* is where I take that leap! I choose *God* this time! Is it going to be hard? Yes, I am *devastated* and my heart is so heavy right now. I want to be angry at Shane for all his wrongdoings, but I am so in love with him still that I am just bawling my eyes out, wishing he would call me. But this is my moment of faith that God has given me to shape up, get it together, get over it, and be the person He wants me to be so He can bless me more than I can possibly even dream of after going through what I have gone through with the man I thought loved me so much. So for you all that have a struggle, just know that *everyone* is dealing with something at all times, even a spiritual book writer like me. I now (or will) have two babies with two baby daddies. I live at home and do not have a job and my savings is almost depleted. I am eight weeks pregnant and need to apply to get a job, but who will hire a pregnant girl? You know what? None of that matters. All that matters is that I put my faith in God and believe everything will work out and be okay, that I will heal from Shane hurting me so much, and I will get a job and move out on my own with my beautiful children. Don't *ever* think that anything is impossible. "If You can? All things are possible to him who believes" (Mark 9:23). You know who says that verse? Jesus. So get out your tears, have your moments of losing it, and let's all put our faith in God and get going for Him! Thank you all for listening to my story and I pray wherever your journey leads you that you never lose the faith!

Here are some amazing quotes I found on Pinterest pertaining to faith:

"If your path is more difficult it is because your calling is higher" (ediblefrog.com).

"Dear God, If today I lose my hope please remind me that your plans are better than my dream." (quoteslife101.net).

"There isn't enough room in your mind for both worry and faith. You must decide which one will live there."—Anonymous

"Nothing can stand against our God. Whatever you face in life, if you will just hold your peace and remain at rest, God promises He will fight your battles. He will make a way even when you don't see a way" (spiritualinspiration.tumblr.com).

"When a train goes through a tunnel and it gets dark, you don't throw away the ticket and jump off. You sit still and trust the engineer. Trust God today no matter how dark your situation. God says, 'You are coming out!'" (ibibleverses.christianpost.com).

"Whenever you don't understand what's happening in your life, just close your eyes, take a deep breath and say God I know it is your plan, just help me through it" (statusant.com).

"Instead of saying, 'Lord I don't know how I am going to do this,' say, 'Lord, I can't wait to see how you do this'" (godfruits.com).

"Don't be afraid, for I am with you. Don't be discouraged, for I am your God. I will strengthen you and help you. I will hold you up with my victorious right hand" (Isaiah 41:10).

"To trust God in the light is nothing, but trust Him in the dark—that is faith."—C.H. Spurgeon

"Faith isn't a feeling. It's a choice to trust God even when the road ahead seems uncertain" (DaveWillis.org).

"God never gives you a dream that matches your budget. He's not checking your bank account, He's checking your faith."—Unknown

"David didn't need to know Goliath's strength because he already knew God's" (Anonymous).

"Man says… Show me and I'll trust you. God says… Trust me and I'll show you" (Psalm 126:6).

Faith:
    (F) Forwarding
    (A) All
    (I) Issues
    (T) To
    (H) Heaven.

(Anonymous)

"Prayer is the key to heaven but faith unlocks the door."—Anonymous

"Faith…it's all about believing, you don't know how it will happen, but you know it will" (Design.love and inspiration.com).

"Faith—it does not make things easy it makes them possible" (Luke 1:37).

"Noah waited 120 years before the predicted rains arrived.
Abraham waited twenty-five years for a promised son.
Joseph waited fourteen years in prison for a crime he didn't commit.
Job waited perhaps a lifetime—sixty to seventy years—for God's justice."

"God prepares leaders in a slow cooker, not in a microwave oven. More important than the awaited goal is the work God does in us while we wait. Waiting deepens and matures us, levels our perspective, and broadens our understanding. Tests of time determine whether we can endure seasons of seemingly unfruitful preparations, and indicate whether we can recognize and seize the opportunities that come our way" (John C. Maxwell).

"H.O.P.E.: Hold On, Pain Ends" (Anonymous).

Here is a song by Katy Perry. It is one of my motivator songs. It encourages faith and has helped me tremendously in my fight to continue living for God.

Rise

I won't just survive
Oh, you will see me thrive
Can't write my story
I'm beyond the archetype
I won't just conform
No matter how you shake my core
'Cause my roots, they run deep, oh
Oh, ye of so little faith
Don't doubt it, don't doubt it
Victory is in my veins
I know it, I know it
And I will not negotiate
I'll fight it, I'll fight it
I will transform
When, when the fire's at my feet again
And the vultures all start circling
They're whispering, you're out of time
But still, I rise
This is no mistake, no accident
When you think the final nail is in, think again
Don't be surprised, I will still rise
I must stay conscious
Through the madness and chaos
So I call on my angels
They say
Oh, ye of so little faith
Don't doubt it, don't doubt it
Victory is in your veins
You know it, you know it
And you will not negotiate
Just fight it, just fight it
And be transformed
'Cause when, when the fire's at my feet again
And the vultures all start circling

B. SWAGZ

They're whispering, you're out of time
But still, I rise
This is no mistake, no accident
When you think the final nail is in, think again
Don't be surprised, I will still rise
Don't doubt it, don't doubt
Oh, oh, oh, oh
You know it, you know it
Still rise
Just fight it, just fight it
Don't be surprised, I will still rise.

Rise and shine, my friends!

With love,
B Swagz :p

Gentleness

"What do you desire? Shall I come to you with a rod, or with love and a spirit of gentleness?" (1 Corinthians 4:21).

Gentleness has a very simple definition: *kindness*. I also want to break the word down further into the word *gentle* which means "compassionate" and "mild."

    I have totally been avoiding this chapter of my book, not the actual act of writing it but writing about the content I am about to confess. This is something I have honestly been struggling with a lot lately, but it has been a problem for many years in my life. Being kind to others is something I find great joy in. I love making a person's day, whether it is a loved one or a stranger in the street. I am blessed abundantly and I abundantly give back to others. While it is extremely easy for me to be kind in this way, I am not always kind in what I say to others, especially when I feel that I am right. You see, I was raised in a family (my mom's half) that has this "I'm right. You're wrong" attitude. Even when I am *wrong*, I must *always* be right. And let me tell you I fully admit that and I absolutely hate it! And when I don't get my way or if someone tells me something I don't want to hear, then I honestly let them have it and revolt to the point of shunning those I love most and blocking them from contacting me. And I do this to the people I love most—my dad, my brother, my sister-in-law, my mom, and the man I love. If they say something to me that presses my buttons in any sort of way, I just snap and I couldn't be meaner about it. It is a horribly wicked evil that comes out of me, but I cannot help but think about what my dad always says when I act like that toward him, "You are just like your mom." He is absolutely right about that, and it kills me to hear him say those words because she is not someone I want to be like. I will not say anything bad about her, except that she has always put herself before me and my brother. Another word for that is selfish, and that is what she is. And that is the woman that raised me for half of my life—the early years, the *important* years. Sadly enough, her mother is like that and so was her husband (my grandpa). My aunt was sort of like that. My uncle was just into mind-altering substances but he died at a young age, so to me he was the just best uncle ever. In this chapter, I want to point out that we need to be gentle in our actions and in our words with others. It sounds so simple to me when I write it, but in the moment, I truly struggle with this immensely.

When I think of the word *gentle,* I think of a newborn baby. Babies are so fragile that we must be ever so gentle with them in the way we hold them, touch them, support them, and comfort them. Most baby products on the market will say the word *gentle* on their label, whether skin products or clothes or blankets. The baby industry promotes this gentleness to infer that your baby will not suffer any harm from their products, just pure gentleness. How comforting for those of us that are moms! It makes me think how can such evil words or acts or gestures come from people that were once gentle, innocent babes? The devil, that is how. He robs us of our innocence, our love, our purity. He disguises himself as pleasure and desire and deceit, but in the end, he causes pain, regret, and turmoil in our lives. I found a set of verses in the Bible that is titled *As Newborn Babes* and find it fitting for this section. It is written by Paul to newborn Christians. The verses say, "Therefore, putting aside all malice and all deceit and hypocrisy and envy and all slander, like newborn babies, long for the pure milk of the word, so that by it you may grow in respect to salvation, if you have tasted the kindness of the Lord" (1 Peter 2:1–3). Long for gentleness, deliver gentleness, and receive gentleness.

I went to the hospital this morning and had corrective toe surgery on my pinky toe that has been causing me a great deal of pain. The doctors, nurses, and staff were so kind, compassionate, and gentle in their actions and in their words toward me. I thought to myself, *Whether someone is ailing or hurt or disabled, we should always treat others this gently.* The nurses were so gentle when putting my IV in, asking me medical questions, giving me take-home instructions. The entire process, I felt nothing but love. I want to feel this way *every* moment of *every* day! I thought of how I could improve of this in my life, not just toward my family members and loved ones but also to everyone I come in contact with. Pertaining to the world, I am quite an aggressive driver with a considerable amount of road rage. I remember reading a pin on Pinterest that stuck with me that I am going to meditate on before every time I drive. It says, "Do not judge. You do not know what storm I've asked her to walk through.-God" (Unknown). I changed the *do not judge* part to *do not be mean.* When

I drive, I tend to tailgate, blow my horn, speed, cut people off, etc. My driving is not godly in the least. I need to remember that quote and be mindful of what kind of day each person may be having. The person in front of me may have just lost their mother, the person to my left may have been diagnosed with a terminal illness, the person to my right may have been in a recent car accident, and the person behind me may have found their boyfriend dead, just as I did in the past. *Every single person* has their own battles. I pray I remember this throughout my day, especially when I am driving! I pray you can recognize your faults, as well, and pray we can all be gentle, kind, and compassionate to every human being (and animal) on this earth. I mentioned this verse earlier, but I will use it again. Jesus says, "A new commandment I give to you, that you love one another, even as I have loved you, that you also love one another. By this all men will know that you are My disciples, if you have love for one another" (John 13:34–35).

I also mentioned earlier that I tend to snap on my closest family members, including my dad, my mom, my brother, and sister-in-law. I don't know how or why I came to be like that. I really do hate it. I know that my brother and I have been like that since high school. It makes me angry even thinking about the rage that comes out of me. Such haste and hostility possess me in my moments of weakness. Life is too short to act so immaturely toward my loved ones. I want to first of all sincerely apologize to them right now and let them know that I am so totally aware that I act like a maniac at times and I am writing this book to fix myself, especially with this chapter. Now that I have apologized, I would like to look at some verses to help me adjust the major attitude problem I have developed so that I set a better example to others and so that I can just be happy and at peace with the people I love.

In regard to the man I currently love (my boyfriend), I truly need to read this chapter to myself on a daily basis to become the gentle girl I once was with him. Regardless of the traumatic events this man has put me through, I forgive him. I have forgiven him so many times I feel like God at moments, handing out forgiveness. It can be a curse, but I absolutely love that about myself. However,

I have not been able to forget these things and it is causing me to be extremely harsh on him, even harsher than he deserves. I had a conversation on the phone with him a few weeks ago and he said to me, "Babe, I am working so hard to get myself better but you don't seem to be making any changes." I said, "I have been praying about my anger toward to you." And just then I figured it all out. I said to him, "Don't you realize that when you pray about something God puts it in your life even more?" As I said that to him, I realized that every time I had gotten mad at this man, it was God giving me an opportunity to correct myself and my actions. My boyfriend always tells me I need to think before I act. He sure is right! I need to recognize the situation, and regardless of how it makes me feel—mad, upset, sad, angry—I need to think to myself, *Okay, B, this is a test from God. Do not let Him down!* And I need to do it 100 percent, no halfway or partway allowed. I sort of did that today. I drove thirty minutes to see him but accidentally followed the wrong directions on my GPS (I typed in Miles Ave. and S. Miles Ave. popped up first). He didn't have a phone for me to call him back on, so when I could not find him, I decided to just turn around and go home and told myself, "Do not get mad at him when he calls, just say that you turned around." He called, and while I told him I was trying not to get mad about it, I still yelled a bit and that is not okay.

I like a quote I saw on Pinterest that says, "Be all in or get all out. There is no halfway" (Unknown). So I decided to write my boyfriend a letter tonight because I can write better than I speak. We recently decided it is best and *necessary* for us to take some time apart so that we can each work on ourselves for the next year. In the letter, I said my main goal is to work on becoming the person God wants me to be, the person writing this book for others. Since we agreed on about a year, we both know that leaves room for others to find me or him as single. I wrote to him that even though that would absolutely kill me, if I have truly changed by the time we reunite this time next year, then my reaction to a new girlfriend would have to be without anger, jealousy, or anything vengeful. After all, if we are meant to be, then we will be together regardless of anything or anyone. Maybe the calmness of my reaction would steal him away from the potential new girl but either way, I want to be that way not just for him or myself but for God. So I vow from this very moment to continue to work on my shortness with him. I shall remember this verse from the Bible written by Paul to the Corinthians for the man I absolutely adore, "Love is patient, love is kind *and* is not jealous; love does not brag *and* is not arrogant, does not act unbecomingly; it does not seek its own, is not provoked, does not take into account a wrong *suffered*, does not rejoice in unrighteousness, but rejoices with the truth; bears all things, believes all things, hopes all things, endures all things" (1 Corinthians 13:4–7).

Coldhearted Christians

I came up with this term myself, but believe me when I say that coldhearted Christians exist. A coldhearted Christian finds pleasure in talking to no one of the world. A coldhearted Christian considers all to be sinners, even some of his brothers (brethren). A coldhearted Christian feels he is always right. A coldhearted Christian judges those of the world (and even those in his church), when it is *God* who is to judge. A coldhearted Christian shows little, if any, forgiveness toward those that have done him or his family wrong. A coldhearted Christian gossips and participates in criticizing those who are talked about in the news, yet considers himself not to be a busybody. A coldhearted Christian shuns you if you drink, smoke, or participate in any impairing activity, even if they themselves experimented with such things in the past. A coldhearted Christian believes he is going to heaven while nobody else has a chance. A coldhearted Christian is a hypocrite but argues with you that you are one. A coldhearted Christian is racist or agrees with racial stereotypes. A coldhearted Christian is selfish and does not want to better anyone, even though he goes to church at every appointed time, learning the gospel (which says to preach the Word of God to *all*). Basically, a coldhearted Christian is just that—cold. They are more judgmental than a drunk person off the street. They do not count themselves as once sinners. They are the biggest hypocrites out there, and they are sometimes the ones sitting in church every Sunday morning. Beware of these Christians! I am speaking this to you because I know them. I live with one—my father.

The Bible warns us of hypocrites. "Or how can you say to your brother, 'Brother, let me take out the speck that is in your eye,' when you yourself do not see the log that is in your own eye? You hypocrite, first take the log out of your own eye, and then you will see clearly to take out the speck that is in your brother's eye" (Luke 6:42). Just because you go to church every Sunday morning and evening and every Wednesday night Bible class does not entitle you to treat others poorly because they are not Christians and because they are not perfect. Jesus was nailed on the cross next to two *criminals!* And He *forgave* one of them upon request. It's funny because people like this seem to *know the Bible so well*, yet they forget some of the most important teachings in it. Number one, God is the ultimate judge (James 4:12). Number two, to love one another. "A new commandment I give to you, that you love one another, even as I have loved you, that you also love one another. By this all men will know that you are My disciples, if you have love for one another" (John 13:34–35). My dad likes to argue that he is only supposed to be nice to other Christians. I beg to differ! This makes me so angry that he thinks this. My brother has also fallen victim to this nonsense. Let me go ahead and write an example of Jesus right now to prove my dad is incorrect. It is when Jesus was sitting with the tax collectors *and* sinners. "As He passed by, He saw Levi the son of Alphas sitting in the tax booth and He said to him, 'Follow Me!' And he got up and followed Him. And it happened that He was reclining *at the table* in his house, and many tax collectors and sinners were dining with Jesus and His disciples; for there were many of them, and they were following Him. When the scribes of the Pharisees saw that He was eating with the sinners and tax collectors, they said to His disciples, Why is He eating and drinking with tax collectors and sinners? And hearing *this,* Jesus said to them, *'It is* not those who are healthy who need a physician, but those who are sick; I did not come to call the righteous, but sinners'" (Mark 2:14–17). Another verse: "But love your enemies and do good and lend, expecting nothing in return; and your reward will be great, and you will be sons of the Most High; *for He Himself is kind to ungrateful and evil* men. Be merciful, just as your Father is merciful" (Luke 6:35–36). One more verse: "Do not judge, and you will not be judged; and do not condemn, and you will not be condemned; pardon, and you will be pardoned" (Luke 6:37).

Up until today, I honestly looked up to my dad because I thought he was the most devout Christian I knew. Sadly, after his attack on the man I love, I no longer see him as a loving Christian, just another hypocrite whose pride has got to him. Maybe he forgets that he once was a drinker and an unfaithful member of the church for more than twenty years or perhaps he forgot when he abandoned my brother and me when he married another woman with two children of her own. He basically replaced us, taking my stepmom's daughters on vacations and to local events without including us. Should I have forgiven him? Yes. Should I hold that grudge against him forever? No. And I don't. I pray he humbles himself before it's too late and realizes the true meaning of what it is to be a Christian.

My brother and I were raised in a *very* conservative church (my mom's side of the family), so conservative that they kicked me out for not attending for a number of consecutive months. I was not perfect, and this church requires perfection. If you miss an appointed time, you must report it and have it announced or the members there will automatically consider you an awful, horrible person. They assume you are skipping on purpose, even if you are mentally or physically ill. This church, to me, is a cult. You know they had the entire church sign a letter of dismissal for me, *including* my *dad* and my *brother*. Those two could not wait to kick me out. They did the same to my mom for living with another man without being married. That is a little more reasonable. I would like to know how many of them had sexual relations before marriage. How many of them lived with their significant other before marriage? How many of them have or had mental issues? Depression? These people are wolves and they are *not* an example for others to be inspired to devote themselves to God. If anything, they drive members *away!* I remember when I would go there I felt like I had to be so perfect or I would go to hell. Would you believe when my aunt died, at her funeral, members of that church came up to me and said, "Honey, you need to come back to church." I said, "I am at a church, a *great* church!" They said, "Honey, you are not at the right church. You will not get to heaven unless you come back to *our* church." I am *not* even kidding that a few of the women said that to me. The nerve! There was also a point in time where we had an amazing bubbly, energetic preacher that I was super close with. After the church let me go, I ran into him at the nursing home where my grandpa was staying. He was sitting on the right side of my grandpa's bed when my grandpa said to me, "Brooke, I really wish you would do the right thing and go back to church." I said, "Grandpa, I will go back to church, but I refuse to go back to *that* church where I feel like if I am not perfect I am going to hell. I am not going to go to a church that feels they are the only people in the world that are going to heaven. I will not be a part of what I feel is a cult." Do you know what that preacher said to me? Nothing! He turned his head and shunned me as if I had cursed the Lord.

Let me tell you… No, wait. Let me show you in the Bible that churches like that are *not* acceptable to our kind and forgiving Lord. "Many false prophets will arise and will mislead many. Because lawlessness is increased, most people's love will grow cold" (Matthew 24:11–12). Yes, you do not have to be friends or hang out with those of the world. God makes that clear. However, God does not say to hate these people and be rude to them and to not forgive them and to shun them and treat them like dirt. Absolutely not! If anyone tells you this, please ask them for book, chapter, and verse, and please email me (BSwagz4God@gmail.com) because I would like to be informed of this information. Simply put, the definition of a Christian is this—a follower of Christ (from my NASV concordance). Remember when I mentioned the WWJD (What Would Jesus Do) bracelets? These coldhearted Christians (particularly my dad, my brother, and their church) need to ask themselves that question before they judge someone that made a mistake and to remember that the *only* sinless person to exist is Christ. And just a fun little fact—that church that I speak of that kicked me and my mom out has increased in its member dropouts with each year. Gee, I wonder why.

If it wasn't apparent to you, I wrote the above out of some anger. I am most inspired to write when my emotions are at peak and when events happen in my life that align with the chapter I am writing. I wanted to make it clear, though, that everything I mentioned above *is* (quite unfortunately) true. My dad and my brother placed an extreme judgment on someone I love so, so much and it really made me question them if they felt they were being Christians. They both agreed that they were, and that is just so sad to see, especially knowing they are my closest family. I also wanted to inform nonbelievers and those that may not have a strong faith that every Christian is not necessarily a good example. Just like there are good and bad people in the world, there are also good and bad Christians. Do not be discouraged by them, for it is just a part of life. Look to those Christians that lift you up and direct you in all situations, *good or bad.* The church I mentioned above is part of the nondenominational group—the Church of Christ. As you can read, it is not a place that I felt encouraged at all but rather *discouraged,* and therefore I chose to find another place of worship. When looking for a church, allow the Bible to be your guide. If the church follows what the Bible says without adding to or taking away from it, then it is probably a church that God would approve of. It does not have to be called *Church of Christ* like some strictly conservative people may think. It may be called *Church of God* or even something else. I was always told that the *Church of Christ* is the *only* church I can attend. That can lightweight be considered brainwashing which cults are known for, so beware of those churches. I encourage you to find a church you see and think you may like and stop in for a worship service. If it abides by the law (the Bible), then it may be the place for you. Remember, every church will have its members that are hypocrites, so don't overlook every church because you will never find one without some coldhearted Christians. Associate with the warmhearted ones and you won't be disappointed.

    One last point and we will wrap this up. I wrote the above about three weeks ago after an argument with my dad. The week after, we had another argument that resulted in me bringing up this section I wrote about him. So today, out of nowhere, my dad decides to bring it up and he tells me how *wrong* I am in my writing. He asked me to back myself up with verses, so I spit about three verses at him and he says, "You are treating the Bible like a storybook." Really, Dad? So I said, "Who is to say that *you're* right in your interpretation? Who is to say *I* am right?" The only true ones that know what they meant when they wrote it are the inspired writers of God. No amount of study Bibles, preachers, priests, or interpreters would ever be able to figure that out *no matter what because we are not God!* My dad has never believed in me, but that is okay. I will not let him break my spirit nor discourage me in writing this book for myself and for you. I mean, it is for people like him, too, but I can guarantee he would never pick it up to read because that is just how he is. No big deal. Life goes on. I know my purpose on this earth is to reach out to others with the Word of God. Not everyone will agree with it. Some people will love it. Some people will hate it. That is just how it goes and I am totally okay with that.

Being gentle toward one another is critical to keeping the peace within yourself and others. If you find it difficult to be kind and compassionate to other people, pray about it. Let God know your weaknesses. He will be gentle on you. If you just can't get yourself to lighten up, change your perspective on who you are trying to please. Instead of being kind to others for *others*, be kind to others for *God*, as He has and will always be kind to you. Remember, everyone has their battles, so put yourself in their shoes before you are unkind to them; it may make it easier.

Self-Control

"And in your knowledge, self-control, and in *your* self-control, perseverance, and in *your* perseverance, godliness" (2 Peter 1:6).

Hold Up

I just looked in my concordance for its definition of self-control. There was none. It is self-explanatory. We need to *control ourselves* in whatever it is that we do to ensure everything glorifies our Father above. We need to show self-control in what we do, what we say, what we wear, who we hang out with, who we love. We need to control our behavior, our temptations, our urges, our struggles. This is a super tough one. Everything I just listed I struggle with. I know you struggle with it, too, as we are all human and fall short of the glory of God. Self-control is not impossible, though, and may be achieved a lot easier when following the Word of God. Think about peer pressure. Why is it so easy to cave? The answer is found in 1 Corinthians 15:33, "Do not be deceived: 'Bad company corrupts good morals.'" Temptation is much easier to give into when we hang around those who practice such things. Solution? Surround yourself with *good* company every day! It really doesn't get much simpler than that. I have cut off many people in my life to get away from the evil deeds they participate in because I, too, was a participant. When I eliminate bad company, my temptations dissipate and the devil seems to flee from me.

We all have a secret life. You know, the life we live when no one is looking. This is probably more of a struggle than the struggles we face while out in public. We *all* have a secret life of some sort. A secret sin, if you will, that we each struggle with. We must find that self-control from within to conquer our demons. We cannot borrow self-control from anyone. It is up to our personal willpower to stay strong against our struggles. Addiction is a great example. I have dated two drug addicts in my life (sad but true). I have tried my absolute hardest to save them, but I realized that no matter what I did for them, I could not fight off their urges to use. That is *their* battle, and they need to find *their* strength to overcome those urges. No amount of good deeds, comfort, money, or gifts can help them overcome. It is up to them! All I can do (and all that I do) is pray for them. I pray they find the strength to overcome and that they find the desire within themselves to do good. An addiction is a true struggle, and drugs are not the only addictions out there that people struggle with. I had an eating disorder several years ago. I went to one inpatient treatment center and one outpatient treatment center and I *still* did not overcome my problem. I had to practice self-control on a daily basis to find the strength within to resist binging and purging on my food. I had to shut out all of the voices in my head calling me fat. I had to resist the scent of fresh baked cupcakes when I walked into the grocery store. What made my addiction *extremely* difficult was the fact that my dad was a chef when I lived with him at the time. He was always baking delicious desserts and cooking rockstar dinners for me. I really had to focus on practicing self-control not in just what I ate, but I had to resist the urge to yell at my dad for cooking awesome, delicious food for me. Of course, I asked my dad to help me out by cooking healthier foods which he did because he is the best dad ever. However, to this day, I have to practice that self-control to resist overeating. It is so super hard, even comparable to the addiction level of heroin because food and heroin release the same feel-good endorphins. I truly empathize with drug addicts and wish them all the success in the world to let go of their habit and practice that self-control from within to resist the urge to use. You know who to turn to. His name is God.

What we say. Let me tell you, I *struggle* with this! Cursing is a huge downfall for me. Again, it goes with who you hang out with. When I was extremely devout to church and church groups and only hanging out with sober people and people of the church, I kid you not, I did not say a curse word for a year and a half!! Mind you, I cursed under my breath when I was alone, but the fact that I didn't speak slander in front of anyone is even beyond me right now. I truly

B. SWAGZ

do not know how I did it but I would like to do it again, especially because I have an eight-month-old son and I want to set the proper example to him. Growing up, I *never* heard my parents say a curse word until I was well into my twenties. They did good, right? You see, outer influences are *so* important! To this day, actually, I have never heard my dad say the *f*-word. He is a man of the church and sets an amazing example to me and my son. The book of Proverbs has some verses in regard to how we speak: "Put away from you a deceitful mouth and put devious speech far from you" (Proverbs 4:24). "A gentle answer turns away wrath, but a harsh word stirs up anger, the tongue of the wise makes knowledge acceptable, but the mouth of fools spouts folly" (Proverbs 15:1–2). "Pleasant words are a honeycomb, sweet to the soul and healing to the bones" (Proverbs 16:24, also my fave!). Words can hurt others, even minus the curse words. We need to be wary of *all* of our words. Proverbs speaks many verses on anger and lying as well: "Truthful lips will be established forever, but a lying tongue is only for a moment" (Proverbs 12:19). "Lying lips are an abomination to the Lord, but those who deal faithfully are His delight" (Proverbs 12:22). "He who is slow to anger has great understanding, but he who is quick-tempered exalts folly" (Proverbs 14:29). "A hot-tempered man stirs up strife, but the slow to anger calms a dispute" (Proverbs 15:18). "He who is slow to anger is better than the mighty, and he who rules his spirit, than he who captures a city" (Proverbs 16:32). I love the book of Proverbs! A word to the wise…watch your words (including me!).

We need to also watch what we wear and practice self-control in resisting the urge to flaunt our bodies. I am obsessed with style and fashion and, of course, my swag! And, I admit, this is yet another flaw of mine. With so many different styles out there these days, not to mention they are bringing back *old* styles (which are, to say the least, a little *more* provocative), it is hard to stay dressed properly. This is a must and let me tell you why. When we dress indecently, we are tempting the eyes of many. I am talking to both women *and* men; it works both ways. "You have heard that it was said, '*You shall not commit adultery;*' but I say to you that everyone who looks at a woman with lust for her has already committed adultery with her in his heart" (Matthew 5:27–28). That being said, whether we are married or not, committed in a relationship or not, we are *all* adulterers for just *thinking* sexual thoughts about another man or woman. While those who look are considered adulterers, then the ones that cause another to commit that sin of adultery are *also* at fault. If we cause someone to lust after us, we are stumbling blocks to them. God does *not* like this! "Woe to the world because of *its* stumbling blocks! For it is inevitable that stumbling blocks come; but woe to that man through whom the stumbling blocks comes" (Matthew 18:7)! We have to be mindful of this, not just for our sakes but for the people that we may cause to stumble. I'm so ashamed and realize right now that I have probably caused a great deal to stumble because of my selfish desire to seek attention from men. Making sure I look my best in clothing that I should not have worn in my past truly disgusts me. I pray to be more conservative in my apparel so that I do not cause anyone to stumble, and I apologize to those that I have caused to stumble and ask your kind forgiveness. I will work on this and pray that if it is something that you struggle with that you can find the willpower to resist the need to flaunt your body but flaunt your faith instead. The main reason I actually came up with this book idea is because I want to start a clothing line someday, but I wanted guidelines from the Lord of how to design the clothes I will sell. So I got my Bible out and stumbled across the basis for this book—Galatians 5:22–23 (the fruit of the Spirit)—and thought to myself that I need to be mindful of what God would want. Shortly after reading that, I stumbled across one of my favorite books of the Old Testament. Proverbs 31:10–31 is titled *Description of a Worthy Woman* in my Bible. I read it and could not believe what I had read. I truly felt as if I were reading about myself when I read verses 24 and 25, "She makes linen garments and sells *them*, and supplies belts to the tradesmen. Strength and dignity are her clothing." That is when I *knew* I was meant to work for the Lord teaching others instead. God truly works in crazy ways! Since then I have come across many verses pertaining to how we (as Christians) present ourselves to others. "Your adornment must not be *merely* external—braiding the hair, and wearing gold jewelry, or putting on dresses; but *let it be* the hidden person of the heart, with the imperishable quality of a gentle and quiet spirit, which is precious in the sight of God" (1 Peter 3:3–4). Specifically to women, Paul writes, "Likewise, *I want* women to adorn themselves with proper clothing, modestly and discreetly, not with braided hair and gold or pearls or costly garments, but rather by means of good works, as is proper for women making a claim to godliness" (1 Timothy 2:9–10). I am so glad I just pointed that verse out, as I truly needed to remind myself of that again. My good works for the Lord, being a spiritual teacher, must reflect in all aspects of my life. See, *crazy* ways!

I also just came across a great set of verses to add to this section and it is titled *Put On the New Self,* starting in the third chapter of Colossians, "Therefore if you have been raised up with Christ, keep seeking the things above, where Christ is, seated at the right hand of God. Set your mind on the things above, not on the things that are on earth. For you have died and your life is hidden with Christ in God. When Christ, who is our life, is revealed, then you also will be revealed with Him in glory. Therefore consider the members of your earthly body as dead to immorality, impurity, passion, evil desire, and greed, which amounts to idolatry. For it is because of these things that the wrath of God will come upon the sons of disobedience, and in them you also once walked, when you were living in them. But now you also, put them all aside: anger, wrath, malice, slander, *and* abusive speech from your mouth. Do not lie to one another, since you laid aside the old self with its *evil* practices, and have put on the new self who is being renewed to a true knowledge according to the image of the One who created him—*a renewal* in which there is no *distinction between* Greek and Jew, circumcised and uncircumcised, barbarian, Scythian, slave and freeman, but Christ is all, and in all. So, as those who have been chosen of God, holy and beloved, put on a heart of compassion, kindness, humility, gentleness and patience, bearing with one another, and forgiving each other, whoever has a complaint against anyone; just as the Lord forgave you, so also should you. Beyond all these things *put on* love, which is the perfect bond of unity. Let the peace of Christ rule in your hearts, to which indeed you were called in one body; and be thankful. Let the word of Christ richly dwell within you, with all wisdom teaching and admonishing one another with psalms *and* hymns *and* spiritual songs, singing with thankfulness in your hearts to God. Whatever you do in word or deed, *do* all in the name of the Lord Jesus, giving thanks through Him to God the Father" (Colossians 3:1–17).

All of that is really a simple concept, do you agree? I like how it says in verse 10, "And have put on the new self who is being renewed to a true knowledge according to the image of the One who created him." Turn to the beginning of your Bible and read Genesis 1:27, "God created man in His own image, in the image of God He created him; male and female He created them." Since God is perfect, He does not cause us to stumble. He created us in His own image and, therefore, does not want *us* to cause others to stumble. He wants us to reflect *His* image and *His* alone. May we all remember who our true example is—our Lord and Savior Jesus Christ. When we get dressed today, we should ask ourselves, "What would Jesus do?" and find the answer to that question in our outfits. Yes, it's hard, but God *never* says it is easy being a Christian. "Enter through the narrow gate; for the gate is wide and the way is broad that leads to destruction, and there are many who enter through it. For the gate is small and the way is narrow that leads to life, and there are few who find it" (Matthew 7:13–14).

Who we hang out with is of *great* importance, as I pointed out earlier in the chapter. Bad company corrupts good morals. This is absolutely 100 percent true. Another verse we can look at is another favorite of mine. In Matthew 6:24, it reads, "No one can serve two masters; for either he will hate the one and love the other, or he will be devoted to one and despise the other. You cannot serve God and wealth." Yes, it is talking about God and money. Let us change the word *wealth* to the word *pleasure*. If we are hanging out with those that are *of the world* and seek evil pleasures and serve themselves with their desires, how likely is it that you will do the same if you hang out with them? Right, it is *not* impossible. For most of us, however, we hang out with those we wish to engage in the same behavior with. Therefore, we must choose our crowds wisely. "Do not give what is holy to dogs, and do not throw your pearls before swine, or they will trample them under their feet, and turn and tear you to pieces" (Matthew 7:6).

Self-control must also be practiced in romantic relationships, whether boyfriend and girlfriend or husband and wife. The urge to cheat on someone can be a huge struggle for many people in both men and women. I have been cheated on before, several times, and let me tell you, if you do not know what it feels like, then you are truly blessed. It is heartbreaking and enraging at the same time. I remember dating a boy when I was seventeen. I wasn't very good at having a boyfriend back then and he was my first real boyfriend. I was very on and off with him, and we rode a roller coaster throughout our two years of dating. I finally got to the point of feeling a real, serious love for him and told him from the bottom of my heart that I loved him. He didn't seem as excited as I thought he would be after begging me to love him on his level for quite a while. It was within the next couple of weeks that I found out he was seeing someone else behind my back. He ended up marrying that girl ten years later. They were married for a total of three years. Then *she* cheated on him. Crazy, right? And in the end, he still wants me back. Lol. I can't help but laugh.

Anyways, there are verses in the Bible that speak on marriage and being devout to one another. "Now concerning the things about which you wrote, it is good for a man not to touch a woman. But because of immoralities, each man is to have his own wife, and each woman is to have her own husband. The husband must fulfill his duty to his wife, and likewise also the wife to her husband. The wife does not have authority over her own body, but the husband *does;* and likewise also the husband does not have authority over his own body, but the wife *does*. Stop depriving one another, except by agreement for a time, so that you may devote yourselves to prayer, and come together again so that Satan will not tempt you because of your lack of self-control" (1 Corinthians 7:1–5). There are also verses speaking to men and women separately about how they are to act in the world so that they don't tempt someone or tempt themselves to commit adultery. "Likewise, *I want* women to adorn themselves with proper clothing, modestly and discreetly, not with braided hair and gold or pearls or costly garments, but rather by means of good works, as is proper for women making a claim to godliness. A woman must quietly receive instruction with entire submissiveness. But I do not allow a woman to teach or exercise authority over a man, but to remain quiet. For it was Adam who was first created, *and* then Eve. And *it* was not Adam *who* was deceived, but the woman being deceived, fell into transgression. But *women* will be preserved through they bearing of children if they continue in faith and love and sanctity with self-restraint" (1 Timothy 2:9–15).

Girls, that is *oh so* important! Don't worry about impressing other men. Be true to your own and to God. My mom still dresses as if she were in high school. She has always been like that. In a way, I am a lot like her. We both crave attention from others, especially boys. But she did this while being married to my dad, my stepdad, and now to her newly engaged boyfriend. But like I mentioned before, I cannot help her with that. She is the only one that can control her actions and her behaviors and how she dresses. I know I want the love of my life to love me like no other so I will not give him a reason not to. Being a new mom now, it is a lot easier for me to practice self-control in what I wear. For one, I don't want to be judged by others as being that mom. That's what my mom did when I was a child, and I find it extremely inappropriate and honestly embarrassing. There is nothing wrong with looking good in a decent way.

In closing, I would like to leave you with this verse: "Let no one say when he is tempted, 'I am being tempted by God;' for God cannot be tempted by evil, and He Himself does not tempt anyone. But each one is tempted when he is carried away and enticed by his own lust. Then when lust has conceived, it gives birth to sin; and when sin is accomplished, it brings forth death" (James 1:13–15). God *never* tempts us. Only the devil tempts us and it is our duty to fight him off with every fiber of our beings! We all desire things we should not because we all fall short of the glory of God. Jesus is the only perfect man in human existence and we cannot blame Him for our shortcomings, but we can look up to Him for encouragement, guidance, and strength. Jesus himself was also tempted by the devil. "But He turned and said to Peter, 'Get behind Me, Satan! You are a stumbling block to Me; for you are not setting your mind on God's interests, but man's'" (Matthew 16:23). Therefore, we must set our minds on godly things. We live in a tough world and it only gets tougher as the years go by as new technologies develop on what seems like a daily basis. Since Jesus was in the flesh as we all are, He was tempted in similar ways that we are today. "For since He Himself was tempted in that which he has suffered, He is able to come to the aid of those who are tempted" (Hebrews 2:18). Pray upon your temptations and your stumbling blocks and ask the Lord to let the devil flee from you and he *will!* "Submit therefore to God. Resist the devil and he will flee from you. Draw near to God and He will draw near to you" (James 4:7-8). Remember the *Faithfulness* chapter and *believe* and *trust* and have *faith* that God can and *will* rescue you from everything it is that you struggle with. I have faith in you, but you have to believe in yourself and the Lord to overcome that evil with good.

Live by the Spirit

"For to me, to live is Christ and to die is gain" (Philippians 1:21).

Live It Up

How many times have you heard the phrase, "You only live once" aka "YOLO?" Dozens for me. As I get more in tune with Christ and His teachings, I am beginning to use this phrase in quite the opposite way. For example, if I am in some sort of peer pressure situation and someone is like, "Oh, come on. YOLO!" I'm thinking to myself, *Yeah, I only live once and that's the life the Lord is going to judge me by, so I better do what is right.* We only have an average of about eighty years to live (that is a guess). By teenage years, we should know better from worse, good from bad, wrong from right. From there, we have, let's say, sixty-five years left of living here on Earth. Since we only live once, don't you agree that it is *so* important to get it right? Maybe we should rephrase "You only live once" to "Heaven or hell?" Living by the Spirit is just that. It is *not* living by man or by what man says. It is living only by what the Lord says. The Bible is our holy guide. It is God's rule book for us here while we are living on Earth. Instead of thinking about the Bible as a *rule book*, I suggest we look on the bright side. How awesome is it that we have a personal guide to get into heaven? God wants us to follow Him and His word because He wants *every single person* on Earth to join Him in His beautiful palace one day. That in itself is a beautiful thought and a more than deserved privilege to each and every one of us.

If God wants us to live by the Spirit, you know the one that *does not* want us to live that way? Satan. Satan will do everything in his power to keep us from doing right. Why? Because he sucks! And if he knows our weaknesses (which he does), he will feed off those to ensure that we are far off of God's path and on path of destruction instead. This is when we must find our strength to resist the evil deeds of the flesh. How? For one, we pray. We ask God to let the devil flee from us to resist Satan's temptations. How else? We need to become aware of our triggers. For example, the people we surround ourselves with can be a major contributing factor to our *giving ins.* The Bible has much to say on this subject. "Do not give what is holy to dogs, and do not throw your pearls before swine, or they will trample them under their feet, and turn and tear you to pieces" (Matthew 7:6). Paul writes to the Philippians, "Beware of the dogs, beware of the evil workers, beware of the false circumcision; for we are the *true* circumcision who worship in the Spirit of God and glory in Christ Jesus and put no confidence in the flesh" (Philippians 3:2–3). Basically, Paul is saying that we need to watch our Christian backs because our godliness can be easily overtaken by our fleshly desires in any given moment. A few more examples of triggers include going to parties or social events, hanging out with people that curse, or staying out late. If attending a party or social event makes you want to drink or do anything else that would be considered inappropriate to our Lord, then cut the parties out of your lifestyle. If hanging out with someone that has a foul mouth tempts you to curse, don't hang out with them anymore. If staying out late causes you to skip Sunday morning church, go to bed early. Whatever the temptation you struggle with, eliminating those triggers is your best bet. Does this mean that our lives are going to be totally boring and unentertaining? Well, that depends how you look at it. If you feel that sin is the only way to enjoy your life because you only live once, then, yes, this lifestyle will probably seem pretty drab to you. However, if you find joy in the smallest things, such as smelling a flower, feeling the sun on your skin, loving every moment, then your life will be amazing. If you are truly concerned with your final destination (heaven or hell), then making the right lifestyle choices won't be such a hard choice for you to make. Remember, it is all about living for *God,* not yourself or your friends or anyone else. Once we get that concept down, these decisions are a lot easier to make.

B's Confession

Right now, at this very moment, I must confess that I am once again struggling with living for God. I don't get it. I do so well and eliminate all of the things (triggers) in my life that aren't godly and I feel great for a few months. Next thing I know, I'm back to chilling with the people that I do not act godly around at all. They don't even know a spiritual B exists because I instantly give in to old habits when I reunite with them. But that is not to say that my friends cause me to fall. When I give in to my old life of sin, that is all on me. I didn't find the strength to resist *my* temptations. What do I do? I need to use God as my shield and do good deeds to keep me from the evil deeds my flesh greatly desires. I opened my Bible today to a random spot and I literally came to this verse: "But I am afflicted and needy; hasten to me, o God! You are my help and my deliverer; o LORD, do not delay" (Psalm 70:5). It is verses like that one that encourage me to get back to living for God. He will help me in every way I ask; to be a stronger Christian and a better example to others. Here are a few more verses to remember when we fall:

> "No temptation has overtaken you but such as is common to man; and God is faithful, who will not allow you to be tempted beyond what you are able, but with the temptation will provide the way of escape also, so that you will be able to endure it" (1 Corinthians 10:13). This verse was written to the Corinthians instructing them to avoid the mistakes that Israel made.

> "Put on the full armor of God, so that you will be able to stand firm against the schemes of the devil" (Ephesians 6:11).

> "Stand firm therefore, *having girded your loins with truth,* and *having put on the breastplate of righteousness,* and having shod *your feet with the preparation of the gospel of peace;* in addition to all, taking up the shield of faith with which you will be able to extinguish all the flaming arrows of the evil *one.* And take *the helmet of salvation,* and the Sword of the Spirit, which is the Word of God" (Ephesians 6:14–17).

So, then, how do we put on the full armor of God? By reading and studying the scriptures which will guide and direct us to righteousness. Also, going to church and surrounding ourselves with those of like minds. Finally, keeping busy! Boredom can cause us to think and even *crave* sin. When we are not busy for the Lord, the devil is busy plotting his next scheme.

I guess the point of my confession is to tell all of you that no one is perfect, not even a spiritual book writer like me. I struggle a lot and I am struggling right now as I write this to you. Ironically enough, my preacher gave a lesson last night that fit perfectly into my life. The lesson was about what Paul wrote to Timothy. "Pay close attention to yourself and to your teachings; persevere in these things, for as you do this you will ensure salvation both for yourself and for those who hear you" (1 Timothy 4:16). Just as Paul says, I need to pay attention to what I do if I am going to teach others so as not to misguide others in their lives. People look to preachers and teachers for a reason—to live by their example. Just as Jesus is our example, I have been purposed of being a spiritual teacher by God and will now live as an example to everyone that crosses my path. I have learned to be more careful in my actions around others so that none of us (including myself) fall short in the end.

Living by the Spirit is probably the hardest possible way to live, but nobody said it was going to be easy. In fact, the more spiritual you are the harder it is going to be because Satan does not want us to live for God. So not fair! Unfortunately, Satan comes in many forms; even our closest friends and relatives could be our biggest tempters when it comes to living the right life for God. These people can really bring you down and some may even hate on you for the way you are attempting to live. I have most of my back tatted with a religious piece. The saying I put at the top of my back says, "Hated by many, Loved by few." Not going to lie, that was originally for my hater fan club. I was young and conceited. Now I use the saying to define my spirituality in reference to this verse: "You will be hated by all because of My name, but it is the one who has endured to the end who will be saved" (Matthew 10:22). Jesus continues to say, "Do not fear those who kill the body but are unable to kill the soul; but rather fear Him who is able to destroy both soul and body in hell" (Matthew 10:28). We cannot worry about not being liked by our friends or family or anyone for that matter. We have to worry about hell, and I don't mean that in a bad worry kind of way. We just need to be aware of that horrifying, dark dwelling place we may end up in if we do not live our lives for the Lord. Being a Christian is tough and it has been like that since Adam and Eve.

One more passage: "If the world hates you, you know that it has hated Me before it *hated* you. If you were of the world, the world would love its own; but because you are not of the world, but I choose you out of the world, because of this the world hates you" (John 15:18–19). Do not be scared. This does not mean everyone is going to hate you. You may not be hated on by anyone. Whether people like us or not, though, we need to follow our Lord and live it up for Him.

B's Favorite Motivational Verse: Always Move Forward

"I press on toward the goal for the prize of the upward call of God in Christ Jesus. Let us therefore, as many as are perfect, have this attitude; and if in anything you have a different attitude, God will reveal that also to you; however, let us keep living by that same *standard* to which we have attained" (Philippians 3:14–16).

Walk by the Spirit

"Therefore be imitators of God, as beloved children; and walk in love, just as Christ also loved you and gave Himself up for us, an offering and a sacrifice to God as a fragrant aroma" (Ephesians 5:2).

Walk It Out

We are finally onto the very last thing that we are told to do in Galatians chapter 5 which is to *walk by the Spirit*. "If we live by the Spirit, let us also walk by the Spirit" (Galatians 5:25). This is kind of like the phrase *practice what you preach*. If you are going to say that you do something yet you *do not* do it, then why are you fronting? There is a word for this—hypocrite. All of us have been hypocrites before in one way or another. If you feel you have never been a hypocrite, then, dang, I'm impressed! Another term we can use for this—front-runner. God does not want us to be hypocrites or front-runners about His word, and when you are a Christian, there are *a lot* of things we are *not* supposed to do. Consider this, even if we appear as perfect to others as we say we are, God knows what we are doing. At. All. Times. So even if we think we are fooling others, there is no fooling God, and, really, there is no fooling ourselves, either. We know what we do. We are consciously aware of our decisions to not do what is right in the sight of God (unless we are mentally ill). Fooling others by putting on a front is only hurting our chances of getting into heaven, not theirs. Do you really want to risk going to hell just so others think that you are perfect? Remember, God loves a humble attitude and He *knows* that living this life is extremely hard… He came here and lived it and saw it for Himself. Walk the walk for you and for God, and if you stumble along the way, well, hey, join the club, be humble, and walk it out again!

Here are a few questions I have for you. Answer honestly.

Do you go to church because you want to?
Do you go to church because you are forced to?
Do you go to church because everyone else does or because you feel you are supposed to?
Are you paying attention when you sit in church?
Do you zone out during church or let your mind wander?
Do you attend church consistently?
Do you only go to church on Christmas and Easter?

When it comes to church, God has pretty high expectations. He tells us which church to go to. He tells us what days to attend. He tells us how church services are to be conducted. He has specific instructions for the brethren. He has specific instructions for the elders. Everything we need to know about church services are taught to us in the Holy word. The Bible provides the sole truth and the *only* instructions we are to follow. As the old saying goes, "If you talk the talk, then *walk the walk!*"

I know how hard it is to be a Christian. As I have pointed out, it is a lot harder to live as a Christian, but the reward in heaven is so absolutely worth it! If you are not a Christian yet, I pray you will consider it. You will be just as tempted as you were in your life of sin (if not more tempted), but spending an eternity in Paradise is the promise we receive by our awesome Lord. Remember, it's *okay* to struggle. We are all human. I just shared my life story with you so that you can see how imperfect I am, even as a Christian. The point of being a Christian is to always move forward and never let the devil win. If you fall, you fall. Just get right back up and walk it out! Not only am I rooting for you, but so is our Lord.

Much love and God bless!

Conclusion

"We count those blessed who endured. You have heard of the endurance of Job and have seen the outcome of the Lord's dealings, that the Lord is full of compassion and *is* merciful" (James 5:11).

I had so many lessons to learn before completing this book, faith being the biggest of all. My dear friends, God does not put us through distress or discomfort or downright difficult things to ruin our lives. It is *the devil* that tempts us and takes us off course, but God *always* gives us the opportunity to escape evil and to learn the lessons we need to learn so that we can live our lives for our Creator, not His enemy. God gives us strength and courage to endure our hardships and to overcome our greatest temptations. He wants us to *wear* love, joy, peace, patience, kindness, goodness, faithfulness, gentleness, and self-control (Galatians 5:22–23). That is the *swagga* God wants us to have. Not merely appearance, but an inner swag that ultimately defines the *swagga of our souls.* The things of this world are the things He does not want us to wear, including immorality, impurity, sensuality, idolatry, sorcery, enmities, strife, jealousy, outbursts of anger, disputes, dissensions, factions, envying, drunkenness, carousing, or things like these (Galatians 5:19–21). Evil *is not* swagga, and that is exactly what that second list pertains to. The devil is determined to sway us away as far as possible from our Lord so that he can take as many souls to hell with him as he can. Why dress for the devil and reap an eternity of suffering when the Lord will reward us with Paradise?

As you have read my personal journey of endeavors, it all really comes down to one thing—endurance. We are *all* faced with difficulties in our lives and we *all* have the decision to live our lives *with* or *without* God. God promises us if we live for Him and endure to the end we *will* be saved (Matthew 10:22). Always pushing forward is the key to overcoming our losses and defeating our weaknesses. Life is hard, but without God, life is not living at all. God puts us through things to learn lessons... *His* lessons. He wants us to learn to *swag* ourselves out with *the fruit of the Spirit*. He gives us this Holy guide so that we aren't captive of the evil deeds of the flesh. *Swagga for the Soul* is about the inside and reflecting that on the outside.

My auntie told me a quote tonight and she said she believed it was meant for her to tell me, "The whole purpose in life is to help others through it" (Unknown). The conversation just before she shared that with me—I told her I am writing the conclusion to my book *tonight* and that everything I have been through was supposed to happen before I completed this book so that I could learn the lessons and share them with others. Life truly is amazing, as hard and as painful as it may seem at times. I know without a doubt that God has brought me to and through everything for a great reason.

I really hope this book has helped you on your journey as it has helped me on mine. May you choose the Lord over the devil and strive for goodness in your life so that you can meet the Lord at those beautiful, pearly gates. God bless you and may God be with you always. <3

Swagga Takeaway

Be stylish. Be weird. Be amazing. Be glamorous. Be golden. Be authentic. Do all these things to glorify God in your appearance, demeanor, attitude, and character. That, my souls, is *swagga*!

Works Cited

Byrne, R. *The Secret.* Hillsboro, OR: Beyond Words Publishing. 2006.

The Lockman Foundation. *New American Standard Bible* (Reference ed.). Anaheim, CA: Foundation Publications, Inc. 1998.

Merriam-Webster's Collegiate Dictionary (10th ed.). Springfield, MA: Merriam-Webster Incorporated. 1999.

Zondervan. *The Zondervan NASB Study Bible.* Grand Rapids, MI: Zondervan. 1999.

About the Author

B. Swagz AKA "B" was raised in an extremely conservative Church of Christ. At age seventeen, she was baptized into Christ and devoted her life to the Lord. After many mistakes and imperfections, she realized being a Christian was a lot harder than it seemed. Being caught up in a world of temptation throughout the rest of her teen years and into her twenties, she constantly battled the devil and always fought her hardest to be perfect, as her church had told her. When B. Swagz failed to have perfect attendance at her childhood church, she was removed as a member by the elders with a signed petition by every member of the church, including her own family members. Regardless of these actions, B. Swagz continued her spiritual journey and was led to a more liberal Church of Christ.

After being a member there for three years, B. Swagz gave birth to a baby boy. Being a single mother and handling her infant son all on her own, her not-so-perfect attendance thereafter estranged her from that church as well.

For the next four years, B was involved in an abusive relationship; had a second baby boy while her boyfriend was in prison; lived on her own; and failed miserably at life. B always knew that God had a great purpose for her and that there were many reasons for her dark and broken past.

Even though she is temporarily without her children, B. Swagz remains faithful in knowing that the Lord will restore to her what she has lost. She uses her personal testimony to reach the souls of the sick and the broken because Jesus says, "It is not those who are healthy who need a physician, but those who are sick; I did not come to call the righteous, but sinners" (Mark 2:17).

CPSIA information can be obtained
at www.ICGtesting.com
Printed in the USA
LVHW041932200523
747567LV00003B/420